CREDIT INTELLIGENCE

Boosting Your Credit Smarts

PRAISE FOR *CREDIT INTELLIGENCE*

"Everything you ever wanted to know (and didn't) about credit cards, purchasing trends, and buying habits. Polly and Mava show you how to leverage credit wisely and effectively manage debt. Informative and fun!"

– Jemma B. Sinclaire, D.C.,
Nutritionist at Essential Nutrition 4U

"If you are going to learn about credit, how to leverage it properly, and how to manage debt, why not learn from the real professionals? Polly's experience and knowledge about the industry from top to bottom can help you position yourself in the best way possible when it comes to handling your credit and achieving financial success in this ever-changing global marketplace."

- Bill Hallock,
Vice President, Keppler Speakers

"*Credit Intelligence* taught me that credit bureau reporting is not consistent and it's my responsibility to verify that the data reported is correct. Accurate data leads to improved financial health."

– Dr. Topher Morrison,
Best-selling author of *Collaboration Economy*

"In the six years I've worked with Polly, she has been 100 percent committed to consumers AND merchants being credit smart. Polly sets her standards high and expects nothing less than world-class service for her clients. This book is a reflection of her 40+ years of payments industry expertise."

- Donny Palma,
Executive VP of Sales and Payment Operations, Pazien, Inc.

"A must-read for anyone who's not regularly reading their credit report and thinks card activity alerts will suffice."

– David Short,
Senior Director Global Operations, Juice Plus+ Company

CREDIT INTELLIGENCE

Boosting Your Credit Smarts

Polly A. Bauer, CPCS & Mava K. Heffler

BALBOA.
PRESS

A DIVISION OF HAY HOUSE

This book includes selected excerpts from the best-selling, award-winning book, *The Plastic
Effect: How Urban Legends Influence the Use and Misuse of Credit Cards*, by Polly A. Bauer
and Stephen Lesavich, ISBN No. 9780983749905, Copyright ©2012 by Coconut Avenue, Inc.
All rights reserved. These excerpts are used with written permission of Coconut Avenue, Inc.

The authors and publisher of this book do not offer any accounting, business, legal,
medical, or any other professional advice of any kind. The intent of the authors and the
publisher of this book is only to offer information of a general nature to assist you in your
quest for a better understanding of the use and misuse of credit cards. In the event that
you use any of the information in this book for yourself, you do so at your own risk, and
the authors and the publisher assume no responsibility for your actions whatsoever.

Balboa Press books may be ordered through booksellers or by contacting:

Balboa Press
A Division of Hay House
1663 Liberty Drive
Bloomington, IN 47403
www.balboapress.com
1 (877) 407-4847

Because of the dynamic nature of the Internet, any web addresses or links contained in
this book may have changed since publication and may no longer be valid. The views
expressed in this work are solely those of the author and do not necessarily reflect the
views of the publisher, and the publisher hereby disclaims any responsibility for them.

The authors of this book do not dispense medical advice or prescribe the use of any
technique as a form of treatment for physical, emotional, or medical problems without
the advice of a physician, either directly or indirectly. The intent of the authors is only to
offer information of a general nature to help you in your quest for emotional and spiritual
well-being. In the event you use any of the information in this book for yourself, which is your
constitutional right, the authors and the publisher assume no responsibility for your actions.

Any people depicted in stock imagery provided by Thinkstock are models,
and such images are being used for illustrative purposes only.
Certain stock imagery © Thinkstock.

Print information available on the last page.

ISBN: 978-1-5043-4202-5 (sc)
ISBN: 978-1-5043-4203-2 (hc)
ISBN: 978-1-5043-4204-9 (e)

Library of Congress Control Number: 2015917228

Balboa Press rev. date: 2/3/2016

Contents

Dedication

Sending our love to some bright stars in our universe that lit the way for this work:

Betty Caulfield. Our hearts know that she continues to be with us both—as mentor, sage, counselor, and teacher.

Polly Matthews. Polly's beloved Aunt who, despite recently transitioning, persists in whispering in her ear.

Daria Heffler. Mava's very loved, intelligent daughter who does her best to keep Mom trendy and young.

Foreword

If you could select "the road to good credit" as a route to program into your GPS, life would be really easy. You could avoid all the hazardous sales sites that require a plastic detour, the purchasing potholes that result in the creation of additional debt, and the shopping accidents that cause you to buy something you cannot live without. You would be able to follow a fortuitous route with turn-by-turn directions and be shown your progress along the way.

Unfortunately, the road to good credit cannot be programmed into your GPS. What if you were able to travel along an informative route with two top executives in the credit card industry who are recognized industry experts, business colleagues, and best friends forever (BFFs)? What if you could be a back seat observer as the "Credit Card Queen" and the "Brand Builder" crisscross the country and are faced with actual temptations that affect their own "credit smarts"?

Let me open the door of that vehicle for you. Sit down and get comfortable in the back seat as you begin your journey. Meet your guides: Polly A. Bauer, aka the "Credit Card Queen" — the former President and CEO of the Home Shopping Network (HSN) Credit Corporation; and Mava K. Heffler, aka the "Brand Builder" — the former Senior Vice President of International Marketing for MasterCard International. With more than three decades of professional experience each, Polly and Mava really know the credit card industry. They are recognized as international experts and top business executives by their peers in their respective professional fields. I am very fortunate to have personally interacted with both Polly and Mava during the course of my legal career.

Your back seat journey begins in the pages of this book, *Credit Intelligence*, as Polly and Mava personally show you how to navigate hazards along the road to good credit—hazards like the effects of credit card debt on your health, relationships, credit scores, and more.

Polly and Mava provide you with personal directions to help you to determine if you are really "credit smart." They assist you in recognizing common credit card traps and credit card advertising techniques that can manipulate your emotions so you make impulse purchases. Through their conversations, personal temptations, and purchasing decisions, they present important credit card topics in a fun and creative way. Polly and Mava assist you in creating a road map that you can follow which will help you make more intelligent decisions about your own credit—something you can program into your own "credit card GPS system" from your driver's seat, if you will, and that you can use to empower yourself and your family.

Polly and Mava share their personal and professional insights in a humorous way which will keep you engaged throughout this book. On your own journey along the road to good credit, you will never have to ask the question, "Are we there yet?"

Stephen Lesavich, PhD, JD

Co-author of the best-selling, award-winning book, *THE PLASTIC EFFECT: How Urban Legends Influence the Use and Misuse of Credit Cards*. Gold medal winner in the Finance/Budgeting Category, 2013 Living Now Book Awards. Founder and CEO of Coconut Avenue, Inc.

Acknowledgments

Many hands make light the work? Not so light, in this case! Speaking of "Credit," we want to dish out plenty to the following saints for all the caring and countless hours contributed in helping make *Credit Intelligence* even more intelligent:

Stephen Lesavich, PhD, JD. Master of the Foreword, attorney, author, friend.

Leslie D. Edwards. Editor Extraordinaire and Detail Wizard.

Amanda Cole. Research Virtuoso. A bajillion facts, stats, sources, notes...

Introduction

What Does "Credit Smart" Mean?

Stein Mart Department Store. Clearwater, Florida.

Polly: *That dress you're trying on looks terrible on you!*

Mava: *But it's 70 percent off, and I already have the shoes to match.*

Polly: *It doesn't matter. That dress does nothing for you.*

Mava: *Polly, we have a party in two hours, and I need to find a dress—now! If I buy it today, AND apply for the store credit card, I'll get an additional 10 percent off.*

STOP! FREEZE FRAME!

What's wrong with this picture?

We'll tell you.

Even as a marketing expert and co-author of this book, Mava was not showing credit intelligence when she almost:

- made a panic purchase,
- bought from want instead of need, and
- applied for another store credit card.

Before we go any further, we would like to introduce ourselves! Polly has over 30 years of experience in the credit industry. Currently, she is a credit consultant, specializing in credit payments solutions for businesses in both the United States and abroad. She is the former President of The Home Shopping Network Credit Corporation. Mava also has over 30 years in the credit industry. Currently, she is a marketing executive, specializing in branding, direct marketing, and public relations. She is the former Senior Vice President of International Marketing for MasterCard International.

First and foremost, we wrote this book for ourselves, because even though we are experts in related industries, as shopping BFFs, we still get sucked into the buying and credit cycle. Then, we decided that this information could help so many people that we had to share it!

As "Olympic level" shoppers who have fallen into and pulled each other out of many of the traps and pitfalls surrounding the use of credit, we decided we had to write a book on how to boost your credit smarts and still keep the fun in shopping.

During our training in our quest for the "Shopping Gold Medal" (which has involved thousands of hours, thousands of dollars, and hundreds of locations), we became aware of behavioral manipulations by retailers that you need to familiarize yourself with to increase your credit intelligence.

We all think we are credit smart! Not true. With changes in technology and payment types, what may have been credit smart in the past may not be today.

In a report released in April 2012 by the Financial Industry Regulatory Authority (FINRA) Investor Education Foundation, "In Our Best Interest: Women, Financial Literacy and Credit Card Behavior,"it states that:

- As many as 60 percent of us carry a balance on a credit card.
- Up to 40 percent of us pay a late fee.
- Approximately 15 percent of us are over our credit limit.
- Up to 15 percent of us take cash advances on a credit card (which is a very expensive loan).
- In contrast, less than 45 percent of us actually pay our credit card balances in full each month.

This book is for everyone!

Whether you shop at Family Dollar or Nordstrom's, are in debt or flush with cash, use cash or credit, can't get a credit card or have several, this book is for you.

Our intention in writing this book was also to write so that everyone could understand the information we share. That's why we included many of our personal stories and experiences, and we wrote this book using straightforward language.

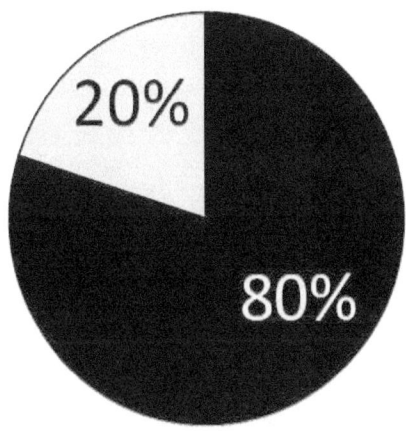

It's also why we approached this book using Pareto's Principle, also called the 80/20 rule. The general idea of this rule is that roughly 80 percent of the effect comes from 20 percent of the cause. For those who are not familiar with this principle, let us give you a brief explanation.

Pareto's Principle originally described the unequal distribution of wealth. In 1906, Italian economist Vilfredo Pareto determined that 80 percent of the wealth and land was owned by 20 percent of the population.[2] This idea was reexamined in the 1940s, when Dr. Joseph Juran observed a universal principle showing that "20 percent is vital and the remaining 80 percent is trivial." He applied this in quality management, where 20 percent of the defects were shown to cause 80 percent of the problems, while the other 80 percent of the defects were shown to be trivial.

The 80/20 rule has become a rule-of-thumb in many industries, being applied from economics to business, management, and computer software issues. For example, 80 percent of software malfunctions, or crashes, have been shown to come from 20 percent of the bugs in the program. Also, in sales, 20 percent of the sales staff will usually generate 80 percent of the sales.

It is important to keep in mind what the vital 20 percent is when managing a problem and to deal with that, so that 80 percent of the problem will be resolved.

In this book, it is our goal to share the vital 20 percent of what, in our experience, is key to know. We think this information will help you 80 percent of the time. We want to share this vital information in a way that efficiently consolidates and communicates a lot of information in one place (and, importantly, takes only 20 percent of the usual time to learn).

It is our hope that this book will boost your credit smarts so you can take better control of your relationship with credit and buying. Then, you can start to control your credit cards instead of allowing them control you—starting *now*.

Even as marketing and credit professionals who know the industry secrets, we still broke the rules many times and fell into the credit card trap. As BFFs on an out-of-control shopping spree, after buying yet another pair of black shoes, we had an epiphany: "There must be millions of people like us, but they don't know what we know about credit and marketing. So, let's tell them about what being credit smart really is, and it will help us, too."

We hope you enjoy the journey the way we have.

Let's look at what being credit smart looks like today. We have created a list of "Smart Tips" in each chapter to provide you with some additional ideas on how to become more credit intelligent. A list of all 85 Smart Tips is compiled in Chapter 12 for your reference.

Smart Tips

You are credit smart when you:

- Pay your balances in full, to avoid paying interest.
- Selectively use your credit card for daily living expenses, to most effectively live within your budget.
- Are aware of your credit score and its accuracy, to maintain your purchasing power.
- Limit the number of credit cards you have and use, to help control your credit score.
- Make your credit card payments on time, to avoid late fees and negative entries on your credit reports.
- Never take cash advances on a credit card, to avoid one of the highest interest rate loans.
- Don't co-sign for anyone else's credit card, to avoid putting your credit history at risk.
- Spend on your credit card today only what you can pay off tomorrow, to avoid getting caught in the "revolving credit card trap."
- Protect your credit card identity and use only secure sources when shopping, to avoid identity theft.
- Buy from need versus want or emotion, to avoid unnecessarily increasing your credit card debt.
- Only take credit cards with rewards or benefits that you need or will use, so that you are not paying extra for perceived rewards.
- Stay aware of your credit card balances, to avoid over limit fees.

At the end of each chapter, we have provided a page for you to make notes about ideas you have to become more credit intelligent. This page is titled "My Credit Intelligence Notes." Since everyone has a different situation, this will allow you to personalize the information you learn in each chapter and refer back to those ideas in the future.

My Credit Intelligence Notes

Chapter 1

Smart Is a Relative Term

6:00 a.m., on the phone while at a payments convention. Boston, Massachusetts.

Polly: *Life in the payments world will never be the same again!*

Mava: *What do you mean? You sound pretty worked up, considering that it's 6:00 a.m.*

Polly: *I haven't been able to sleep. I was sitting in the middle of the convention yesterday listening to the card associations, payment processors, merchants, and software vendors all arguing over the recent government regulations to keep costs down, and everyone is only concerned about their own interests.*

Mava: *So what's new about that? Everyone always has their own interests at heart, and it's never been about the consumer.*

Polly: *This is a day for the record books, girlfriend. Since the first credit card was issued back in 1962, the government has not intervened and actively taken control to stop escalating credit card costs, until now.*

The banks are panicked over the money they'll lose, the processors are scrambling for new revenue streams, and the merchants are confused by all this contradictory information.

Mava: *So what's the bottom line, Polly?*

Polly: *More than ever, the consumer needs to understand how to be credit smart—NOW!*

What you might think was credit smart yesterday is not credit smart today.

And you are not alone.

Remember when you were so proud of making a large purchase on a zero percent interest rate card and only paying $33 a month? Not smart!

Here's the reality: the economy has shifted, card offers are changing, and it costs you more to buy on credit than ever before.

Your interests and the bank's interests about how you use credit cards are at odds.

It's in your best interest to pay off your credit cards in full each month. However, it's in the bank's interest (and it's how they make their money) when you do *not* pay off your credit card in full each month. In fact, we've overheard some bankers refer to customers who pay their balances in full as "deadbeats," because pay-in-full customers can end up costing the bank money because they do not pay monthly interest rates on outstanding balances. You should be aware that banks still make money from these customers on transaction fees and other fees that are not paid by the consumer.

Believe it or not, banks sometimes penalize these pay-in-full customers by lowering their spending limits and increasing their annual percentage rate (APR). At the same time, banks sometimes reward people who do *not* pay off their credit cards each month by increasing their spending limits.

Your interests and the interests of merchants are sometimes at odds, and sometimes they are aligned.

It's in the merchant's interest to have you accept their store credit card offer (if they have one) and to encourage you to spend a lot of money on their store-branded card. Many times, you get a high line of credit as an incentive. All of that makes you feel like a VIP in that store, further encouraging you to spend more money. Sometimes, they try to further sweeten the pot by making the credit card a platinum or gold card, which carries additional shopping privileges and private, in-store shopping events.

Why?

Because when you use their card, the store makes more money.

It's important for you to know that if you take the store card, it can also lower your credit score. This is because it's an additional line of credit against your name, *plus* it usually has a high interest rate, both of which tend to lower your credit score. See Chapter 6 for more information on how your credit score is calculated.

An alternative and potentially smarter strategy would be to use your debit card, as it has no negative impact on your credit score, nor does it drive up recordable debt. Of course, care must be taken to not spend more money than you have, or you may likely be charged overdraft fees. Overdraft fees do not negatively affect your credit score unless you get sent to collections for non-payment of these fees, but the amount you pay for them can be considerable. If you decide to use your debit card on a regular basis, you should familiarize yourself with the laws governing fraud involving debit cards, since you potentially have greater liability with debit cards than credit cards. See Chapter 2 for a discussion about the differences between debit and credit cards.

Your interests and the interests of credit card issuers are sometimes at odds, and sometimes they are aligned.

It's in the interests of the banks and companies that issue credit cards to get you to buy, buy, buy, and to do so using a credit (or debit) card instead of cash.

To facilitate your purchase on one card or another, the card issuers do two major things:

1. They create numerous card product options so that you can choose credit and/or debit cards.

2. They spend millions of dollars on advertising each year that focuses on rationalization, positive emotions, and incentives for you to buy on both a credit and a debit card.

A key job of the credit card issuers is to get you to think that the smartest thing for you to do is always spend on plastic.

Now you can see why we said that "credit smart" was a relative term at the beginning of this chapter.

We recommend that you make note of the following tips.

Smart Tips

You are credit smart when you:

- Pay your balances in full each month.
- Don't take a store credit card just because you are offered a one-time percentage off of your first purchase.
- Use your debit card versus your credit card for most daily living purchases. Remember to keep track of purchases on your debit card so you don't get charged overdraft fees. Be aware of the differences in fraud liability for debit cards versus credit cards (discussed in Chapter 2), and monitor your statements closely for fraudulent purchases.
- Be aware of the APR on your credit cards, how and when your credit card statement cycles, and when your payment is due.
- Compare credit card rewards and benefits. Know what each card is really costing you.

A key goal of credit card associations, merchants (those that have their own credit card), and issuing banks is to get you to buy on credit instead of using cash. In the next chapter, you will learn about a number of card types that are available to you.

My Credit Intelligence Notes

.

Chapter 2

Not All Payments Are Created Equal

Polly's kitchen table. New Port Richey, Florida.

Polly: *In all the excitement of writing this book and with our sixty years' combined experience in the payments industry, we can't take for granted that our readers have access to the same information that we do.*

Mava: *You're right. I think it's important to explain the various types of cards and how each one of them impacts our lives each and every day.*

Polly: *The average consumer carries six different cards in their wallet. Consumers need to know which card to choose for a purchase and how it affects their financial health.*

Mava: *This is especially important if you choose a credit card, as it can have the longest-term impact on your finances. Understanding the differences between credit and debit is really important, too.*

Polly: *So, we're in agreement. This book will focus on using credit intelligently. Understanding the differences between different types of plastics lays a foundation for doing so.*

The information in this chapter provides an overview of the many payment types available to you. Read through this chapter, and then look in your wallet to see what types of cards you carry and use most frequently. Think about whether you should alter your purchasing habits now that you have an understanding of how each type of card can affect you.

Credit Cards Explained

Credit cards use the bank's money to purchase merchandise and services, with payment expected from you the following billing cycle. To be considered for any credit card, an issuer (who you submit your application to) will perform a credit check to determine your creditworthiness.

MasterCard and Visa are card associations that have partnerships with issuing banks. The issuing bank receives your application and approves you for a card under either brand. MasterCard and Visa are brand companies that own global networks. These payment networks can move transactions initiated by the consumer through various levels of processing to the bank that issued the consumer's credit card, resulting in settlement back to the original merchant where the merchandise was purchased. MasterCard and Visa do not issue credit cards. Issuing banks issue credit cards.

Unsecured and Secured Credit Cards

The following excerpt from Polly's book, *The Plastic Effect*, discusses the differences between unsecured and secured credit cards[3]:

> Most credit cards...are *unsecured credit cards*. An unsecured credit card does not require any collateral (e.g., money or property) be secured before the card is issued and used.
>
> A *secured credit card* is a credit card that requires collection of some type of collateral before use. The most common type of collateral is money in a designated account (i.e., a savings or money market account). When money is deposited in the designated account, the amount of money on deposit becomes your credit limit on the associated secured credit card account.
>
> Unlike an unsecured credit card, a credit limit on a secured credit card may be variable. You can request an increase in your credit limit by depositing more money as collateral. Sometimes the issuing bank

will reward a good payment history by increasing your credit line to an amount above what you have deposited as collateral.

The secured credit card is used just like an unsecured credit card. Purchases are made, credit card bills are sent, payments are made, and on-time or late payments are usually reported to the credit bureaus.

Your available credit limit can also vary if you do not pay your charges in full each month.[4] ...

This is similar to making a minimum payment on an unsecured credit card and carrying a balance forward to the next billing cycle, which causes you to pay interest and lowers your available credit limit.

[...]

If you have applied for an unsecured credit card and your application has been denied, you can use a secured credit card to build your credit so you will eventually become eligible to apply for and obtain an unsecured credit card again.

Charge Cards

While the terms credit card and charge card are used interchangeably, they are not the same. American Express, Discover, Diner's Club, and JCB are card companies. All of these companies are both the brand and the charge card issuer. You must apply for a charge card just like you would a credit card.

It is important to know the differences in the companies that issue charge cards. American Express is widely recognized as the number one global travel card product and is accepted at retailers worldwide. American Express charge cards typically have higher limits, require an excellent credit score, and would require a higher-than-average household income to be approved for this type of card. American Express primarily issues paid-in-full cards. Recently, American Express has become very active in issuing a revolving card product that doesn't require you to pay the balance in full in 30 days. Discover is a strong brand that offers widely accepted, revolving card products. Discover is mainly a US product, and it is famous for its cash-back annual rewards. JCB is recognized as a global card brand. JCB is used extensively for travel, is accepted by large merchants internationally, and has become a very strong brand in the United States in recent years. Diner's Club was one of the first cards offered to the public and is one of the oldest cards in existence. It is widely used by military and government associated cardholders.

If you have a paid-in-full card with any of these companies, the good news is that you will never pay interest, but you will be required to pay an annual fee for the privilege of carrying the card.

Rewards Credit Cards

Often marketed as "the more you spend the more you earn," rewards cards encourage you to put purchases on your credit card in return for frequent flier miles, cash back, and/ or merchandise discounts. Only apply for and utilize rewards-based credit cards if you will actually redeem the rewards on a routine basis. See Chapter 4 for an in-depth discussion of this topic.

Affinity Credit Cards

An affinity credit card has an agreement between the issuing bank and a designated partner organization. Every time the card is used, a percentage of the transaction fee is paid to the partner organization. This partner could be a charity, college or university, not-for-profit organization, or sports team. This type of card is excellent for showing your support to an organization you believe in. If you use this card regularly for certain purchases, you can help this organization all year long.

Debit Cards Explained

Often called a check card, debit cards deduct each purchase from the money you already have in an account that is linked to this card. When you return home from shopping, there are no payments to make. A debit card has a PIN that enables you to pay for a transaction out of your account. Because most debit cards are issued with a Visa or MasterCard logo, you can also use your signature to authorize the purchase. The two authorization methods have different costs to the merchant you are purchasing from. Debit transactions cost the merchant less to accept, and banks often show these purchases instantly as pending withdrawals. For convenience, the financial institution that maintains your checking account enables your debit card to be used in ATMs.

As Polly explains in her book, *The Plastic Effect*, one of the most important differences between credit and debit cards is the consumer's liability for fraud protection under federal regulations.[5] Debit cards are regulated under a different law than credit cards, and the fraud liability protection is *very* different. You need to be aware that if you detect fraud on an account associated with a debit card, you need to report it immediately. If you report loss or theft of your card or unauthorized transactions immediately, you have zero liability. If you fail to report an unauthorized transaction within 60 days after any statement listing the unauthorized use is mailed to you, you may be responsible for an *unlimited* financial loss, including all of the funds in your account, any overdrafts, and any overdraft fees that may have been incurred.[6] Guard your debit card and your PIN number closely, and monitor your statements regularly to protect yourself from potential fraud.

Reloadable Cards Explained

Reloadable cards deduct your transactions from a stored value associated with your card. These cards are often referred to as prepaid cards; however, some prepaid cards are not reloadable. This type of card was not included in the consumer protections provided by the CARD Act of 2009,[7] so there are numerous fees to users. There may be fees for initial purchase, activation, reload (deposit), ATM withdrawal, monthly maintenance, PIN transactions, and online bill-pay. If any problem arises with the funds on the card, some reloadable card companies charge per call to access customer service representatives by phone. The following are two types of reloadable cards that you may encounter.

Reloadable Cards

Reloadable cards utilize previously stored funds to make purchases. Some bank accounts offer a reloadable card for cardholders that allows them to stay secure while shopping online. These cards have a purpose, but buyers must be aware that there are no industry regulations on fee structure. Only a handful of prepaid card issuers insure your funds through the FDIC.

Payroll Cards

Employers with a large number of workers find payroll cards to be a great alternative to cutting paper checks. Just as with other reloadable cards, payroll cards can be used to make purchases that debit the transaction from a stored value on the card. The majority of payroll cards carry MasterCard and Visa logos, and they can be used wherever these cards are accepted. Many of these cards don't have reloading fees, because money is deposited directly onto the cards. Recently, some tremendous benefits have become associated with payroll cards. One type of benefit offered with some payroll cards is insurance programs. Another example of these benefits is discounts at local retailers such as gas stations, grocery stores, and movie theaters. Also, some drug stores and fast food restaurants offer rewards programs to payroll cardholders.

Gift Cards Explained

Everyone loves receiving a gift card. When the envelope is too heavy to just be a card, we get excited—wondering where the gift card is from and what item on our wish list we will purchase with it. Did you know that there is more than one type of gift card?

Store Branded Gift Cards

You open the envelope to find a card that has a particular retailer's name on it, without a card association logo. This type of gift card is called a closed loop gift card. It comes with a pre-determined value and can only be used at one retailer. Store branded gift cards generally do not have an expiration date or monthly inactivity fees for the first 5 years. They also do not have an activation fee.

Widely Accepted Gift Cards

You've hit the jackpot when you open the envelope to see the gift card has a card association logo like Visa or MasterCard on it. This is practically free money, right? These gift cards, which can be spent virtually anywhere, are considered open loop gift cards. These cards have a preset value, which is determined by the purchase. Once these funds are used, the card cannot have additional value reloaded to the balance. These cards may have fees designated by the issuer. These fees may be required to be paid by the purchaser (over and above the value of the card), but sometimes must be paid by the recipient (out of the card's total value). You should be aware that an open loop gift card has an expiration date, typically five years after purchase. Inactivity fees may also be charged.[8]

Regardless of the type of card or the benefits associated with it, cards are here to stay for the next few years. You need to understand the types of cards available to you to make credit intelligent choices.

Smart Tips

You are credit smart when you:

- Don't forget to look in your wallet to see what cards you carry and use most frequently.
- Evaluate your own credit smarts and reflect on your purchasing behaviors.
- Understand what cards you use every day.
- Decide which cards best fit in your life.
- Understand that there are different types of cards and know what benefits come from each type.
- Don't accept every card you are offered in the mail.
- Budget how you are going to use each type of card you have in your wallet.
- Know what your bank ATM limits are and communicate to your bank if your needs change.
- Leave balances available on your cards for rainy days or emergencies.

Your emotions and the manipulation of your emotions by other people are affecting your purchasing behavior in ways that you may not realize. The next chapter discusses ways that marketing and advertising strategies attempt to influence your emotions to get you to make purchases you might not make otherwise.

My Credit Intelligence Notes

Chapter 3

Emotional Buying: How Your
Emotions Are Being Manipulated
to Make You Spend More

After eight hours of shopping. International Mall, Tampa, Florida.

Polly: *Ok, so here's our story, and we are sticking to it. All of this stuff in the trunk is yours.*

Mava: *I can't believe we shopped for eight solid hours!*

Polly: *I called my husband three times to tell him we are stuck in traffic, rather than admit that we were still shopping.*

Mava: *They did it again! We got sucked into nine more clearance sales. It seemed like we went to every store today, but, boy, did it feel good at the time. What a rush! We have so much fun shopping together!*

Polly: *Let's get real. We knew what they were doing to us. But how could we resist, when everything was below wholesale cost and every store offered us another 15-20 percent off if we took their store credit card?*

Mava: *I know we started out today saying we had to be strong because we know the whole world was against us when it comes to helping us to not buy. It just didn't work out that way today.*

We are just two of millions who sometimes buy on impulse, buy on emotion, or buy because we can't pass up a good deal, and then are afraid to be honest about it.

There are a lot of complicated emotions surrounding buying. Emotions are a key fuel in the cycle of buying and debt.

Unfortunately, decisions surrounding buying that you might think are yours are not always yours, because they are manipulated by the actions of others. You need to be aware that your buying decisions are being influenced by many other sources. These influences are so powerful that even credit and marketing professionals like us can fall under their spell.

It's time for us to expose these manipulative techniques and make some sense of how you are being affected when it comes to buying and credit card debt. We want to teach you how your emotions are being accessed and manipulated by banks, credit bureaus, credit card companies, retailers, and marketing companies.

Barbara Thau, reporting for *DailyFinance,* reinforces the point about the power and prevalence of impulse purchasing in her article, "Buy Me: 7 Ways Stores Get You To Make An Impulse Purchase,"[9] when she writes, "Retailers rely on a host of tactics to get you to purchase stuff you don't want, don't need and never intended to buy." She goes on to say, "And their ploys often work." The article refers to a behavior study by the retail branding firm The Integer Group, which found that nine out of ten shoppers make impulse purchases, buying items that weren't on their shopping lists.

A few of the tactics used by retailers to get you to buy that Thau shares in her article are:

- "Color-Coordinating Displays": A display showing an entire room makeover may entice you to buy the whole thing, instead of just the one item you actually need.
- "Hitting the Motif of the Moment": Retailers are aware of trends, and they set up displays to lure you into buying items that feature the latest trendy thing.

Shoppers end up buying extra things they don't need and will use only until the next fad hits the shelves.

- "Product Demonstrations": Friendly sales people draw you into a demonstration, showing you an item you may have never noticed otherwise. Debt piles up quickly, because it is likely that this item was not on your shopping list.
- "New and Improved!": Retailers highlight the new season's clothing or the newest smartphone in a beautiful, flashy display in a location that you can't miss. These displays try to make the clothing or smartphone you bought last season look outdated. This plays on your emotions.

There are even more tactics used to get you to impulse buy. Stores hire consultants who study how consumers shop, and they use these habits to design the floor layout and create appealing displays.

For example, in the article "7 Shopping Secrets Retailers Won't Tell You," author Naomi Mannino[10] shares these tactics and more:

- "The 'Magic' of the Display": Visual and verbal marketing strategies are used in displays to make the product more appealing.

- "The BOGO and 2-Fers": Sometimes these can be a good deal for consumers, but many times they are not.
- "Why Clearance Racks are Messy": Retailers know that most shoppers are in a hurry and want well-organized racks of items to buy. The clearance area is often poorly organized on purpose because the store wants you to get frustrated and head to the areas that are well-organized and more expensive.
- "The Influence of Shopping with Your Friend": As we have found, having a friend to shop with can be dangerous if they cause you to spend more than you budgeted. A friend who balances your bad habits, however, can be a good asset to staying within your budget.

Do any of these tactics sound familiar to you? Have you ever fallen for any of them? We certainly have. Never in our lifetime have people been so recession-weary and so totally disillusioned with corporations and institutions that they've previously trusted. These tactics are part of the reason we wrote this book—to teach you to be aware of them and learn how to shop more wisely.

The list goes on!

Another tactic that you may or may not be aware of is "Fake Sales." These have been (and continue to be) created by a number of big name and reputable retailers. In some cases, these retailers have been taken to court.

A fake sale is when a store marks up something very high and then drops the price steeply, creating a perceived discount. By doing so, the store makes shoppers think they're getting a great deal.

This practice is discussed by ABC News Consumer Correspondent Elisabeth Leamy in her article "How to Watch Out for Fake Sales."[11] She explains, "Some stores put a high regular price on an item then deeply discount it to make customers think they are getting a bargain." Leamy also says, "Retailers have always played games to get our greedy little hearts going."

Another type of fake sale is when a merchant offers limited inventory for a short time. For example, an advertisement for reduced price electronics indicates limited quantities. This creates a sense of urgency. Another example of a fake sale is when a store has a going-out-of-business sale, but remains in business afterwards.

We've bought into many of the above tactics. We continually try to stay on top of our impulse buying and to stay credit smart by understanding how our emotions effect our buying.

What we do know—and want you to understand after reading this—is that emotion is a key fuel in the cycle of buying, credit, and debt.

Furthermore, when the cycle of buying, credit, and debt spins out of control, the result wreaks havoc on many lives. The results of financial mismanagement can vary, depending on the circumstances and the size of the problem created. The problems created can range from difficult to catastrophic. Each of these situations creates new sets of emotions, as well as new credit and debt scenarios.

For instance, at a recent corporate conference, Polly was shocked when an internationally-known keynote speaker and author shared her personal story of wanting the satisfaction of feeling gorgeous in a sequined gown, which drove her to make a big investment in herself—spending $10,000 for the garment. She had no idea that by the time the credit card bill came she wouldn't have the funds to pay for it. She told Polly that the short-term gratification that she experienced when she felt so good on stage was not worth all the stress and negative emotions she endured later while trying to fix the credit problems that resulted from this impulse buy.

No one is protected from emotional buying. It impacts and always has impacted all walks of life, all income streams, all demographics, all ages and genders.

Here is a list of questions that might help you to identify if you are making an emotional purchase the next time you buy:

- Am I buying this item to make me feel better or to cover up a hurt?
- Am I buying this item to impress the Joneses?
- Would I buy this item if I were using cash?
- Will I feel the same when the credit card bill comes as I do now?
- Am I buying this to reward myself and/or punish someone else?
- Do I buy emotionally on a regular basis?

Stop for a minute to consider your purchasing habits:

- Identify five emotional purchases you've made on a credit card in the last 90 days.
- Write down the emotions that led you to buy and the emotions you had after purchases.
- Do you see a pattern?

For the purchases that you just listed that left you with negative feelings, can you think of what you could have done instead of buying something or shopping? For example, sometimes the two of us will choose to go on a healthy walk around the neighborhood or to sit with a cup of coffee and talk for hours instead of going on an expensive shopping trip.

We didn't ask you to list your recent emotional purchases in order to make you feel bad or guilty. We are not even saying that all emotional purchases are bad. Saving, budgeting, and planning to be able to afford an emotional purchase can be a healthy and exciting experience. We are talking about unplanned and unbudgeted purchases.

What we are talking about—and what we want you to know—is that the decision to make a number of unplanned, unbudgeted, emotional purchases on credit and debit can be influenced by highly trained experts. These experts make a lot of money and their income depends on you buying what they are selling.

These experts target you with their messages, which appeal to your emotions. You're up against "Sales Guerrillas" who are trained to know what drives emotional buying and how to tap into those emotions at a deep level. You're also up against companies that spend billions of dollars and deploy many powerful techniques in an effort to attempt to influence your buying behavior.

Radio commercials in your car, TV commercials in your home, ads in your mailbox, signs when you walk through stores, sales calls to your home, billboards on the side of the road, emails in your inbox—it just doesn't stop, from the moment you open your eyes until you fall back asleep. The messages we get 24/7 are buy more, buying will make you feel better, get this and you will be happier, buying our brand will make the Joneses jealous...but at all costs buy, buy, buy.

Doesn't all of this sound like what would be described as brainwashing? It is!

Along with the act of buying come emotions, ranging from pleasure to guilt.

And how do most of us buy? We use credit cards—sometimes too quickly, easily going into too much debt. With this debt comes an additional range of emotions, which we refer to as the vicious cycle.

If you are visual like we are, the following chart will help you understand the vicious cycle even more.

Emotions are at the center of it all.

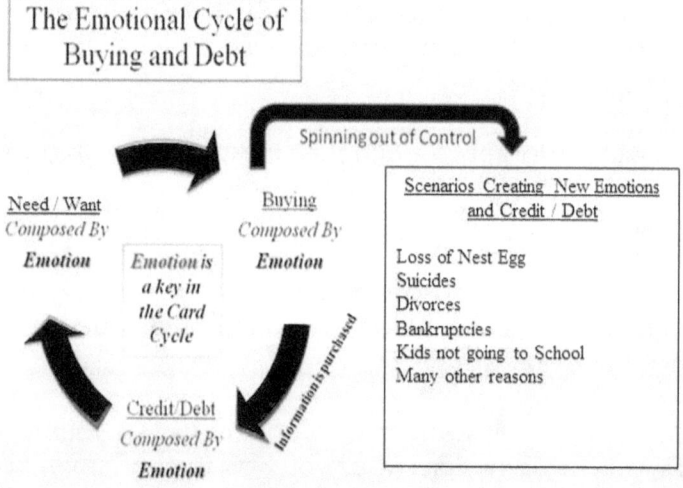

This chart shows that when you have a need or a perceived need, you are inspired to buy. When you buy using a credit or debit card, your product purchase information is often sold to credit card marketers, retailers, and/or manufacturers' firms. They start sending you direct mail and email solicitations to create in you additional perceived needs, playing on emotions such as:

- joy
- jealousy
- pride
- fear
- depression
- guilt
- stress
- doubt

- entitlement
- happiness
- loneliness
- need
- inferiority
- lack
- high self-esteem
- low self-esteem

Recent research has shown correlations between types of emotions and the type and level of spending. These relationships can be quite complex.

In the article "When Self-Esteem is Threatened, People Pay with Credit Cards," *ScienceDaily*[12] cites a study, which concluded that "people shop for high-status items when they are feeling low and that they are more likely to make those expensive purchases on credit."

In that article, *ScienceDaily* cites research conducted by the London Business School and Cornell University. This research found that people whose egos were threatened by being told that they had performed poorly on a task (regardless of the actual results) were more likely to consider purchasing luxury goods than people who were told they did well on the test. This group would also be more likely to make such a purchase with a credit card. This research concluded that buying on credit would be more likely "because actually parting with cash can be psychologically painful."

Emotions after buying may include:

- guilt
- worry
- embarrassment
- doubt
- shame
- emptiness

At some point this cycle creates more new scenarios. When it gets out of control, the things that may occur have even greater consequences associated with them—such as suicide, divorce, bankruptcy, kids not going to school, loss of a nest egg, health problems, and more.

We are going to share ways that you can reverse this cycle of negative emotions in Chapters 8 and 9. When you take control of your credit debt and your finances by being credit intelligent, you should have a whole new perspective on your life! Instead of having all these negative emotions, you should feel positive about your choices. Positive emotions have a strong effect on many areas of your life. You may see your relationships improve and may find improvement in your health as well. Over time, your credit intelligent choices should become second nature to you. Your new credit intelligent habits should make you feel good about yourself and you should feel good about your credit intelligence.

Smart Tips

You are credit smart when you:

- Identify how you are feeling emotionally when you buy on your credit card.
- Stop and ask yourself when buying an item, "What is driving me emotionally to buy this?"
- Realize you are making an emotional purchase, and instead, take the same money and save it towards your dreams or goals.
- Don't spend any more on your card than you would pay with cash.

In the next chapter, we will continue to show you how to raise your credit intelligence by being savvy about credit rewards programs.

My Credit Intelligence Notes

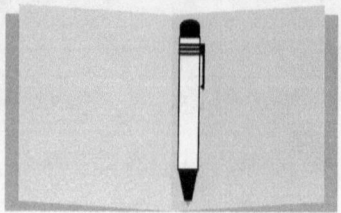

Chapter 4

Rewards Are Not Always Rewards: How to Make Your Credit Cards Work for You

Hartsfield-Jackson Atlanta International Airport. Atlanta, Georgia.

Mava: *I don't believe this! Have you noticed that there are four credit card kiosks with marketers in just this one terminal? They're all shoving their card offers down people's throats that offer miles and free tickets if they apply today.*

Polly: *What's sad about that is that most people have no idea that getting another credit card negatively impacts their credit score.*

Mava: *Everyone is looking for a deal. We've become a 'Groupon' society. That's all they're thinking about.*

This scenario is very common in today's economy. Credit card companies are appealing to the consumer's desire for instant gratification, additional value, and a range of other emotions to persuade them to apply for and use their credit cards.

Shh....

Secrets of Credit & Sales

What credit card companies and banks don't want you to know is that by applying for and obtaining multiple cards, you will lower your credit score. That "free" airline ticket or other reward you were intending to earn enough points for (or spend enough money on a particular credit card for) may very well end up costing you more than you expected.

Many people who have a rewards card end up using the card more frequently, only to discover that the restrictions for obtaining the rewards may make it difficult to actually collect the reward. Additionally, many people don't even bother to apply for the rewards because of loopholes, hassles, blackout dates (in the case of airline miles), and many other reasons. This is called "slippage."

Credit card companies make millions of dollars a year on cardholders who are paying for benefits that they think they will use, but never do. Surveys of consumers have repeatedly shown that a high percentage of rewards cardholders—as high as 40 percent or more—rarely end up using their rewards.

This is another area where it is important to be credit intelligent. Polly and Mava suggest that you not be one of the many people who are paying for rewards cards that you don't or won't use.

It's easy to assess your current rewards cards or any potential rewards cards you are offered by taking a few key considerations into account, including:

- **Get the cash back rules.** All things being equal (such as interest rates and annual fees), cash back rewards do not have the downside of points or airline rewards, which often go unused. With cash back rewards, you can take the money and buy airline tickets or an item you'd like, or you can donate it directly to a charity of your choice. Some cash back rewards cards have no annual fee, so you won't have to worry about spending enough to make more in rewards than you paid for the fee.
- **Check the credit card interest rate and then be honest with yourself about how you pay your credit card.** Credit cards that have rewards programs often have higher interest rates to help the credit card companies fund those programs. Therefore, unless you pay off your credit card bill in full each month, you could end up paying more in interest fees than you could ever earn in rewards. Polly and Mava suggest that you think carefully about signing up for a rewards card with a higher interest rate just for the purpose of obtaining the rewards unless you know for sure you will be paying off your credit card bill every month.
- **Do what's right for you.** If you don't travel or don't plan to do so, then perhaps a cash back rewards card (which has rewards based on purchases made for your home and everyday spending) would better suit you than a card that has airline miles as a reward. How much do you think you'll be spending on a credit card each year in the near future? When you consider that amount realistically, what is the potential value of the

rewards you could earn from the rewards card you have in mind? Of course, you must take into account any annual fees and any anticipated interest charges. By evaluating your spending habits in this way, you should be able to determine if reward cards are credit smart for you and, if they are, you should be able to make a credit intelligent choice if you apply for a rewards program.

- **Don't spend just because you have a rewards card.** Mava and Polly have done more than their share of shopping and justifying purchases made because "it's on sale." However, we strongly advise against spending on a rewards credit card for the express purpose of "earning" enough points to redeem those points in order to get a particular item. This is a bad idea for a number of reasons. The most important reason is that, by doing so, you may spend as much money to earn those rewards as you would have if you had simply bought the item.

Brand loyalty does not always make you credit smart.

We have seen on numerous occasions that the status and loyalty of spending on one brand in order to get rewards and benefits often costs people thousands of extra dollars a year, resulting in limited or no added value. Even Polly has fallen victim to this.

Polly has been card and airline brand loyal for the purpose of earning millions of miles with her favorite airline. Yet, when she needed to get a flight to a speaking engagement in Prague, she couldn't obtain an airline ticket utilizing any of those millions of miles she had earned—even though she tried to book the flight six months in advance. The response of the airline was, "Thank you for being a multi-million miles flyer, but we have very few flights for mileage rewards. We can offer you some point certificates to buy merchandise from our catalog." Unfortunately, Polly had booked many flights with this airline when she could have flown on less expensive flights through other airlines because she thought the million mile status would give her better flight rewards. In this case, Polly's brand loyalty cost the price of a flight to Prague.

Reward incentives are not new. Remember S&H Green Stamps from years ago, and how your grandmother earned a toaster when she opened her own savings account at the bank? Reward incentives these days, however, involve layered partnerships and built-in tactics that, in the end, result in a high percentage of slippage or non-use of the rewards.

Smart Tips

You are credit smart when you:

- Don't overspend today to earn rewards tomorrow.
- Don't accept rewards offers and credit cards that you do not need or will not use.
- Track your earned rewards and use them before they expire.
- Ask yourself, "What is this reward really costing me?"
- Read the fine print on reward offers before you accept the credit card.

In the next chapter, we will discuss how your purchases are tracked and how the information is used to influence you to spend more. By being aware of these practices, you can change how you react and become more credit intelligent.

My Credit Intelligence Notes

Chapter 5

Guess Who's Watching You Buy: Why?

Mohegan Sun Casino. Montville, Connecticut.

Mava: *You are the only person I would drive for four hours to meet for a one-hour lunch.*

Polly: *I guess I know you love me. This is a perfect day for me – lunch with my BFF and slots machines a few feet away.*

Mava: *I love the slots machines too, but I hate knowing I'm being watched and knowing that I'm going to be hit up by credit card offers from the casinos after we leave.*

Polly: *You're going to get a lot more than credit card offers. What about the free room, meals, incentives to return, and the gift shop discounts?*

The people watching you from the ivory towers at casinos are not the only ones watching every move you make. Nearly everything you buy with your credit card and debit card is also being tracked.

Not only is what you buy being tracked, but also when you buy it, where you buy it, and how much you spend.

Much of this information is available for sale to the Sales Guerrillas we previously mentioned. This helps them get even better at targeting you with messages that will persuade you to use your credit card.

Sometimes, even experts like us have to remind ourselves about all this information tracking and laugh when we talk about going out into the world to do errands, realizing that the whole world is watching us.

Charles Duhigg explains this in more detail in his *New York Times Magazine* article, "How Companies Learn Your Secrets."[13] He states, "Almost every major retailer, from grocery chains to investment banks to the U.S. Postal Service, has a predictive analytics department devoted to understanding not just consumers' shopping habits but also their personal habits, so as to more efficiently market to them."

The frightening reality is that a number of companies and agencies can and do buy information about you that includes everything from your job history to the magazines you read; from what topics you talk about through social media to the brand of coffee you drink.

For anyone who goes to a mall, you might be surprised by what Ashley Lutz and Matt Townsend had to say in their article, "Big Brother Is Watching You Shop."[14] They wrote, "To get a better understanding of their customers in real time, mall operators are monitoring shoppers' behaviors with devices that track mobile phone signals, while retailers are finding new uses for old tools such as in-store security cameras. The goal is to divine which variables affect a purchase, then act with Web-like nimbleness to deploy more salespeople, alter displays, or put out red blouses instead of blue."

You may not know it, but when you buy pet items, it is very likely that you will be added to a list of people who have pets, and that list will get sold to a company that markets to pet owners. As a result, you will be bombarded with marketing messages that tell you to buy more pet products and special offers for even more pet products and pet accessories. You could potentially be offered a special credit card that could have a photo of your pet on it.

The gifts you buy and the gifts you receive are also being watched.

Polly's kitchen. New Port Richey, Florida.

Mava: *Oh, wow! I have a Keurig coffee machine, too. When did you get yours?*

Polly: *Last week. A good friend gave it to Frank and me for our anniversary, but here's the weird part. I got this gift, and then I was suddenly inundated by all kinds of offers from coffee companies and accessory outlets. I have no idea how they knew I got this gift.*

Mava: *I'll tell you how they knew! It's not just the buyer's information that is tracked; the gift recipient's information is also tracked. It's like a 2-for-1 deal, because the marketer, the credit card company, and the retailer got both the buyer's name and purchase information and your information, too.*

This story relates how, in this time of recession-weary consumers and businesses, something very interesting is happening. People are craving relief more than ever, even if it's in the form of a little luxury like a machine that makes an espresso instead of just regular coffee.

And here's the kicker. Not only are people's buying patterns being tracked, but what they buy for other people is being tracked, too.

In fact, one of the largest Internet marketing companies in the world has become very successful by using this technique as one of its important marketing strategies.

It's truly you against thousands of highly trained Sales Guerrillas. Companies are spending millions of dollars to keep this sales force in training, teaching them psychological tactics to touch your emotional hot buttons at a deep level. The salary and employment status of this sales force depends on being successful at getting you to spend.

Everything marketing companies do—from the words on the outside of a direct mail envelope that a bank sends to you to the subject line of an email—is carefully tested and calculated. Millions of dollars are spent hiring thousands of experts to figure it all out and execute it in an effort to entice you to take action and buy more. Words, images, and entire campaigns are designed to push your emotional buttons. These emotional buttons include urgency, fear, uncertainty, insecurity, and envy.

The reason we want you to know you are being watched is because what you buy and how you buy is driving companies to create campaigns to tempt you to buy even more and go deeper in debt. When you are aware of this, you become more credit intelligent and you'll likely find yourself reacting differently to these tactics.

Smart Tips

You are credit smart when you:

- Are aware of all of the solicitations you receive in the mail, by email, and by phone.
- Are aware of recent purchases or purchase patterns that you believe triggered the solicitations you receive.
- Notice how you feel when you're bombarded with solicitations, whether they are for donations or are solicitations to buy cars or perfume.
- Understand that what you are buying and how you are buying is being tracked.
- Can link solicitations you receive with your purchasing methods and what you bought.
- Don't accept every store's frequent purchase cards.
- Don't fill out any online surveys.
- Don't give your email address to stores or restaurants.
- Check the box at the bottom of applications and warranty cards saying you do *not* want any future promotional materials.
- Think twice before you click on a pop-up offer when online and/or use a pop-up blocker on your internet browser to prevent these offers from appearing.
- Delete cookies (which are small files that are stored on your computer when you visit a website) from your computer on a regular basis to decrease the amount of information that can be tracked by websites while you are on the internet. This is a simple thing to do. If

you don't know how, you can do a search on how to delete cookies from the internet browser that you use.

In the next chapter, we are going to explore a very important topic—your credit score. This chapter includes the basics on how a credit score is calculated, how your credit score can affect your finances, and ways that you can manage your credit score and maybe even improve it!

My Credit Intelligence Notes

Chapter 6

To Be Credit Intelligent, It Is Critical to Know the Basics of Credit Scores

Dinner at Gino's Pizza. Chicago, Illinois.

Mava: *So, how are all the radio interviews going?*

Polly: *Great, but there's a lot of anger and confusion around finances.*

Mava: *What's the buzz? What are people mad about?*

Polly: *It's a really confusing area, which is made worse by people being unaware of how their credit scores are impacting their everyday lives.*

In order to be credit intelligent, you need to be aware of what's impacting your buying power—for instance, your credit score. You need to be aware that your credit score is based on the information contained in the credit reports from the three major credit reporting bureaus. An important first step is taking responsibility for the information that is currently on your credit report. The information that is being reported to the credit bureaus includes information about your purchases, the number of credit cards you have, and your payment history.

As Polly has found through talking to people who have called into her radio interviews, a surprising number of people are unaware of and afraid to look at their credit scores. If you are avoiding looking at your credit score and are feeling afraid and embarrassed as to what you might find, you are certainly not alone. To be credit intelligent, it is a necessity that you know your credit score. You should also know that there are steps you can take to improve it. In her keynote speech, *"You Are Not Your Credit Score,"* Polly emphasizes that most people become too emotionally involved with this issue, and they connect their identity with their credit score. Most people let their credit score take control of them versus them taking control of it.

In this chapter, we want to demystify what you think about your credit score and also to empower you so that you can release any stress you have associated with your credit score. We also want to teach you how to improve your credit, increase your buying power, and decrease your expenses. Your credit score impacts you in many ways, because credit scores are not just being reported to or looked at by banks. Other organizations—such as mobile phone companies, utility companies, insurance companies, landlords, and government departments—are able to report information to the credit bureaus and to review your credit score.

Now you see what all the fuss is all about, and why we are going to teach you step-by-step what a credit score is. We will also give you some tips on how you can take more control of your credit score.

As we were writing this chapter (a coincidence?), Mava's phone rang, and it was a credit card company offering her another platinum card because she has a high credit score. She declined, which is one of the reasons she has a high credit bureau rating; specifically, she limits the number of credit cards she has. As you raise your credit score, you will be getting more offers, too. Like Mava did, we recommend that you also decline most of these offers, limiting the number of credit cards you carry. Mava was also credit intelligent in her choice to not apply for a credit card through a phone call she received—this is a fairly common way that people are scammed.

Let's start by simply defining what a credit score is:

A credit score is a three-digit number that represents a person's creditworthiness.

This number is based on a statistical analysis of a person's credit files. These files primarily contain credit report information sourced from credit bureaus. Creditworthiness is a term used to indicate how likely you are to repay money lent to you.

Institutions that you might ask to lend you money or give you credit (such as credit card companies and banks) use credit scores to evaluate the possible risk of lending money to consumers and to mitigate losses due to bad debt. Lenders use credit scores to determine which customers they want to give a loan to (e.g., who they deem qualifies for a loan), at what interest rate, and the limit of the amount they are willing to loan. Lenders also use credit scores to determine which customers are likely to bring in the most revenue.

A credit score is different than a credit report. A credit report reflects your credit activity and history.

The major credit scoring system used in the United States is called FICO (Fair Isaac Corporation). This system involves a complicated statistical calculation that combines a lot of your purchase and payment data and history. Most lenders use FICO. The credit score number it calculates for a person ranges from 300 to 850. Later in this chapter, we will show how these numbers impact your ability to obtain credit and loans.

A credit score is calculated by weighing information in your credit report.

The following table illustrates how, in general, a credit score is calculated.[15]

Credit Score Components	
Payment History	**35%**
Credit Utilization	**30%**
Length of Credit History	**15%**
Types of Credit Used	**10%**
New Credit Obtained	**10%**

The following section is an abbreviated version of how FICO calculates credit scores using the categories in this table. This section includes advice from Polly and information from one of the most straightforward explanations that we've seen, by Lee Ann Obringer in her article "How Credit Scores Work."[16]

Credit Score Breakdown

Although the exact formula for calculating a credit score is proprietary information owned by Fair Isaac Corporation (FICO), here's an approximate breakdown of how it is determined:

- **35 percent** is based on your payment history.
  - How many bills have been paid late?
  - How many bills were paid on time?
  - How many bills were sent out for collection?
  - Are there any bankruptcies?
  - The more recent a negative item is, the worse the impact will be on your overall credit score.
- **30 percent** is based on outstanding debt and the percentage of your available credit that is being used (this is referred to as credit utilization).
  - Your credit utilization is a ratio of how much debt you owe to how much credit you have available. A low ratio is considered more desirable to lenders. This factor includes your credit utilization for each of your credit cards individually and an aggregate credit utilization for all your credit cards together.[17]
  - How much do you owe on car loans?
  - How much do you owe on home loans?
  - How many credit cards do you have that are at their credit limits?
  - The more cards you have at their limits, the lower your score will be.
  - Polly recommends that you keep your card balances at 15 percent or less of their limits to improve the credit utilization component of your credit score.

- **15 percent** is based on the length of time you've had credit, referred to as your credit history.
    - The longer you've had established credit, the better it is for your overall credit score.
    - The older the average age of your accounts are, the better it is for your credit score.
    - More information about your past payment history gives a more accurate prediction of your future actions.
- **10 percent** is based on the types of credit you currently have.
    - It will help your score to show that you have had experience with several different kinds of credit accounts, such as revolving credit accounts and installment loans.
- **10 percent** is based on new credit obtained.
    - Opening new credit accounts will negatively affect your score for a short time.
    - If you close older accounts at the same time as you open a new account, the average age of your accounts will decrease. This will affect your credit score for a longer time than if you just open a new account.
    - *Hard inquiries* reported on your credit report in the last two years will have a negative impact on your credit score. Hard inquiries are those you've given lenders permission to make.
    - *Soft inquiries*, which include looking at your own score, have no effect on your credit score.

The Three Major Credit Bureaus

To help you make sure that your score is correct and consistent across all three credit bureaus, you need to be familiar with your credit report from each of these credit bureaus. They are: Experian, TransUnion, and Equifax.

These three credit bureaus each calculate your credit score based on the FICO scoring method. You may notice that your score may be different at each of the three bureaus. This is because each credit bureau calculates its own scores, and the information contained on each of these credit reports may differ. Sometimes, a creditor will report to one credit bureau but not all three.

Lenders may also use their internal or proprietary scoring methods, which may include information like your income, how long you've been at the same job, etc. These scores may be different from the credit bureau scores.

We suggest you order a free copy of your credit report from each of the three major credit bureaus once a year.

You can order your credit report online or by mail. Polly and Mava recommend that you order a credit report from one of the three major credit bureaus every four months. This will allow you to monitor your reported information closely throughout the year. This will allow you to take action on an error in a timely manner. You can easily access your credit reports through a free website run by the federal government: www.annualcreditreport.com. You can obtain one free copy of your credit report each year from each of the three major credit bureaus though this site.

Here is contact information for each of the credit bureaus:

Equifax:

www.equifax.com
P.O. Box 740241
Atlanta, GA 30374
(800) 846-5279

Experian:

www.experian.com
P.O. Box 9530
Allen, TX 75013
(800) 203-7843

TransUnion:

www.transunion.com
P.O. Box 6790
Fullerton, CA 92834
(800) 916-8800

We recommend that you check your credit reports for errors. If you notice information that is incorrect, you should take the following actions:

- Follow the directions specified by the credit bureau that prepared the credit report with the incorrect information.
- Quickly submit a request online or by mail to correct the incorrect information.
- Specify which information you think is inaccurate, and why.
- Include any documents that support your argument.
- Make a request in writing that the information be corrected or removed from your credit report.

- Keep copies of the requests you submit to have the inaccurate information corrected.

You should know that:

- The bureaus must investigate your complaint, usually within 30 days.
- The bureaus must respond in writing. The response will be sent by mail if you send a written request or by email if your request was made online.
- If the credit bureau investigation results in a change in your score, you will be sent a free updated credit report.

It's important to know where your credit score ranks.

The table below will help you see where you stand in the different credit rankings that banks and lenders use to make credit decisions.[18]

Credit Score Ratings	
Credit Score	**Description**
760-850	Excellent
700-759	Very Good
660-699	Good
620-659	Fair
580-619	Poor
Below 579	Very Poor

Credit Scores, Ratings, and Characteristics

Credit Score 760-850: Excellent Credit Rating

A credit rating of "Excellent" is associated with the ability to successfully manage finances. It is characterized by the following:

- a long credit history
- no or few late payments, collections, liens, judgments, or bankruptcies
- multiple lines of credit established
- several different types of credit, such as installment loans and revolving lines of credit
- generally, a stable work history
- will have no trouble securing virtually any loan
- viewed as:
  - An A+ borrower who will receive the very best interest rates, repayment terms, and lowest fees available.
  - Someone who will pay insurance premiums and loan payments on time, and who does not pose great risk.
  - Someone employers view as responsible and less likely to steal from the company or commit fraud.

If you have this credit score rating, congratulations! This is the credit score rating that most people strive to achieve.

Credit Score 700-759: Very Good Credit Rating

A credit rating of "Very Good" is also associated with the ability to successfully manage finances. It is characterized by the following:

- a long, distinguished credit history with responsible payment history
- the ability to handle multiple types of credit responsibly
- for the most part, regarded in the same standard as borrowers with excellent credit history except there may be a higher debt-to-income ratio
- viewed as:
  - For the most part, to lenders, insurance companies, and employers, this person is viewed the same as and will receive the same treatment as anyone with an excellent credit rating.

- In some cases, this person may end up paying a little more in interest than someone with an excellent credit rating, but having a "Very Good" credit score rating will qualify this person for some of the best deals around.

If you have this credit score rating, you should be pleased! You have demonstrated good management of your finances.

Credit Scores 660-699: Good Credit Rating

A credit rating of "Good" is associated with good management of finances. It is characterized by the following:

- this person built a solid credit history by working hard to keep accounts in good standing
- there may be a late payment or two somewhere in the past
- there might be a collections account reported, but it has been paid off
- may have some extra credit card debt, but has made strides to get it under control
- viewed as:
  - Generally, lenders will have no issues loaning money to someone like this. A good credit score will land competitive interest rates and low origination fees, although not as good as the rates offered to a person with a few more points on their score.
  - This person will have no trouble getting an insurance policy for just about any need, but should expect premiums to be somewhat higher than for those with excellent or very good credit.
  - This credit score should not have any negative effect on ability to get hired, although some employers may pass this person by for an equally qualified candidate with a better score.

If you have this credit score rating, it is nothing to be ashamed of. If you have a few negative items on your credit report, they will affect your score less as time passes if you continue to keep your accounts in good standing. With a little time and credit intelligent choices, you will likely be able to raise your credit score into the "Very Good" credit rating level.

Credit Score 620-659: Fair Credit Rating

A credit rating of "Fair" is associated with some problems surrounding the management of finances. It is characterized by the following:

- hit a few speed bumps in the past—late payments, collections accounts, and maybe even an aged public record dot this credit history
- perhaps there is simply too much debt
- viewed as:
    - This person will have a harder time finding a lender willing to service a loan than someone with a higher credit score, especially if the low credit score is a result of slow payments. This score represents a higher risk of default to a lender, and therefore, this person may be required to secure the loan with a down payment or tangible personal property.
    - Unsecured revolving credit will be very difficult to come by.
    - Insurance companies will tend to price insurance policies higher for people in this credit category due to the potential for nonpayment of premiums or the higher-than-average risk for committing insurance fraud.
    - Some jobs may not be available to applicants with fair credit scores, such as jobs in the financial sector.

If you have this credit score rating, you have some work to do in order to get yourself back into good financial shape. It is imperative to take steps now to prevent any additional damage to your credit report and get back on the road to good financial health. If you take steps to reduce credit card debt, ensure that you get your bills paid on time every month, and pay off any open collections, your credit score should improve within several months. It may also help to review your credit report for errors and, if you find any errors, dispute them in a timely fashion. With these steps, your credit score may increase enough during the next three to six months to get you back into the realm of a "Good" credit rating.

Credit Score 580-619: Bad Credit Rating

A credit rating of "Bad" is associated with problems surrounding the management of finances. It is characterized by the following:

- not a pleasant experience—multiple credit issues in the past, most likely involving the payment history on one or more accounts
- also most likely had an account or two in collections, and possibly had a bankruptcy filing
- viewed as:
  - It's going to be extremely difficult to find any lenders willing to lend to someone with this credit score rating without a significant down payment or collateral to secure the loan against default.
  - Insurance agencies will still underwrite insurance policies for this person, but the products will be limited, and they are going to cost significantly more than the same products for customers with better credit scores. There may also be higher automobile insurance costs.
  - Employers will be reluctant to hire someone with this credit score due to the appearance that this person is irresponsible with money. They may also believe that there is an above-average risk of employee theft or fraud, making it very difficult to change positions or get a promotion with the current employer.

If you find yourself with this credit score rating, it's time to roll up your sleeves and get real about your current financial situation. Though your current position may be of no fault of your own due to a job loss, illness, or other unforeseen circumstances, it's your responsibility to take the necessary steps to reverse the course you are on.

Take a long, hard look at where you are in your life. You should take the necessary steps to reverse the trends that led to your "Bad" credit score rating. You may benefit from credit counseling. The National Foundation for Credit Counseling (NFCC) is a non-profit network that can refer you to a member in your area for credit counseling.

Credit Score 579 and Below: Very Bad Credit Rating

A credit rating of "Very Bad" is associated with major problems surrounding the management of finances. It is characterized by the following:

- more than likely is delinquent on more than one account
- likely has active collections accounts
- probably has at least one judgment, repossession, or bankruptcy on file
- if this person has credit cards, they are likely maxed-out or have been shut off for nonpayment
- viewed as:
  - This credit score will have many negative effects on this person's life.
  - Lenders (with the exception of those who specialize in lending to borrowers with bad credit) will not approve this person for any loan product, even if a sizable down payment or collateral can be provided.
  - Insurance agencies will likely refuse coverage based on the risks posed.
  - Often, employers will not hire this person whether there is another viable candidate or not.

If you have this credit score rating, you should take a long, hard look at where you are in your life. You should take the necessary steps to reverse the trends that led to your "Very Bad" credit score rating. You may benefit from credit counseling. The National Foundation for Credit Counseling (NFCC) is a non-profit network that can refer you to a member in your area for credit counseling.

Your credit score translates to purchasing power. Banks and other lenders look at this score to determine whether you qualify for a mortgage or other loans. It also affects your ability to be approved for credit cards and the terms and interest offered to you.

Our intention is to help make you credit intelligent by making you aware of some items that require a specific credit score or range.

Home mortgage rates vary by your credit score. According to Bankrate.com, "A credit score of 740 or more should qualify for the best mortgage rates from most lenders. Depending on the lender, the mortgage rates offered to the highest and lowest credit tiers can vary as much as a full percentage point and a half..." Furthermore, buyers with a FICO score below 620 are not likely to be offered a home loan at all.[19]

Automobile loan interest rates are also greatly affected by your credit score. *Credit.com News* reports that there can be a 10 percent difference in the rates offered to someone with an Excellent or Very Good credit score versus someone with a Very Bad credit score.[20]

Now that you have some insight into how your credit score affects your buying power, let's look at how you might be able to improve your score.

There's hope! There are ways you can raise your credit score.

The good news is that, no matter what your credit score is at the moment, you can still improve your standing among lenders and improve your credit score.

Here are some credit intelligent actions that can potentially improve your credit score:

- Make all your credit card payments on time.
- Pay more than the minimum required amount on your credit cards each month.
- If possible, pay all credit card balances in full.
- Keep each of your credit card balances below 15 percent of the credit limit.
- Review your credit card and bank statements on a regular basis.
- Dispute any charge that does not appear to have been made by you in a timely manner by contacting the bank that issued the credit card.
- Don't apply for a credit card in order to obtain a one time "deal" (e.g., 10 percent off of the current or next purchase).
- Keep your oldest credit cards and refrain from frequently applying for new credit cards.
- Do not take a cash advance from your credit card.

- Check your credit reports on a regular basis for potential errors made by creditors. Take prompt action to remove any inaccurate information from your credit reports.
- If you're given the option to pay for an item in payments, consider saving for the purchase instead. Think about the consequences of a new loan being reported against your credit score.
- Be very careful about accepting offers of "90 days same as cash." Before you accept any offer, get the facts and read the fine print! Find out if the 90-day loan reports into your credit bureau score during the 90-day time frame.

Smart Tips

You are credit smart when you:

- Create and stay on a monthly budget.
- Avoid frequently applying for new credit cards and loans.
- Keep your oldest credit cards active. If you can, avoid closing credit card accounts you've had for a long time.
- Monitor your credit score and credit reports regularly.
- Pay your bills on time. This includes medical bills and utility contracts such as cell phones, cable bills, or satellite network contracts.
- Have at least 3 to 6 active accounts in different categories, i.e. major credit cards, gasoline cards, store cards, etc.
- Minimize the number of store credit cards you have in your name.
- Keep your credit card balances low. Paying down your credit card balances is a great way to help your credit score.
- Pay off your credit card balance with the highest interest rate before paying off lower interest rate balances. Continue to make payments on all of your balances to avoid damage to your credit score. After you have paid off the balance with the highest interest rate, take that amount and apply it to the balance

with the next highest rate. By doing this, you will be amazed how quickly your balances will be paid in full.

- Make more than the minimum monthly payment required on your credit cards. Paying only the minimum amount each month will actually lower your credit score.

My Credit Intelligence Notes

Chapter 7

There's No Free Lunch
and There's No Quick Fix:
Beware of Credit Repair Agencies

Interstate 95. Outside of Orlando, Florida.

As Polly and Mava are driving to Sea World, Polly's cell phone rings. Polly's friend, Eileen, is crying hysterically, believing she had been scammed by a credit repair agency that promised to improve her credit score. What was upsetting her was that her 2008 SUV had blown the engine just after she paid off the loan, and she couldn't buy a new car until she improved her credit score. Polly hung up, shaking her head.

Mava: *What was that about? Is everything okay?*

Polly: *You remember my friend, Eileen. She called two months ago to tell me she had hired a credit repair agency to perform a quick fix to her credit score, so her score would be high enough for her to buy a car.*

Mava: *In this day and age, why would she bite on that offer?*

Polly: *Eileen heard about it on the radio, and their slogan was that they guarantee an improved score and a quick fix. She had a misconception that a third party could do more than she could do to fix her credit. I wish she had talked to me before she had signed up for the service. That's $5,000 down the drain.*

Eileen is not the first person who has bought into the idea that she could buy her way into a higher credit score.

To be credit intelligent, you need to be aware that credit repair agencies cannot guarantee you a quick fix to your credit report and improve your credit score.

There is nothing that a credit repair agency can do to improve your credit report that you cannot do yourself. Even though their actions may result in a temporary improvement in your score, the financial investment is usually not worth the result.

The scam most frequently used by credit repair agencies is to bombard the credit bureaus with disputes that, while under investigation, can possibly create a false, temporary improvement in your score. Once the disputes initiated by the credit repair company are investigated and proven to be inaccurate, the credit score decreases back to the original, lower credit score.

The credit repair epidemic is further exposed by numerous articles, case studies, and testimonials found in print and across the Internet. We have heard these stories over and over. The storylines of all these situations end as follows: "Does this sound too good to be true? Well, it is."

Shady credit repair agencies/organizations seek out and often victimize people that need help; people who are uninformed, vulnerable, and unsuspecting. These organizations also look for people who are struggling with bankruptcy, have credit issues, or are not credit intelligent.

Polly's friend paid $5,000 with the hope that one of these companies could help her get a car loan. Many other people have also been fooled into paying hundreds or thousands of dollars to credit repair agencies to help them get a job, a home mortgage, insurance, or more. Usually, the only thing they get is deeper in debt, and their credit score may actually get worse! The money spent on the credit repair scam would have been better spent paying down debt. It is no wonder the Federal Trade Commission (FTC) has received scores of complaints from consumers about these organizations and has been investigating and prosecuting scammers.

We do not want YOU to be one of the people that are scammed! We want YOU to be credit intelligent.

As opposed to credit counselors (who are qualified to provide guidance on improving your credit reports and scores through better financial management), credit repair organizations claim to be able to remove negative information from your credit report.

Generally, there are three steps to the service that credit repair organizations offer:

1. They ask you to forward to them copies of your credit reports. Usually they request reports from the three major credit reporting agencies (Equifax, Experian, and TransUnion), which you must obtain directly from those agencies.
2. They recommend items on your credit report that you should dispute.
3. They contact the credit reporting agencies to challenge questionable items on your credit reports.

We want you to understand what the credit repair agencies really can do and what they *can't* do. Here are a few things you should know to provide additional perspective as to why you have *more* power than you might realize, and why the credit repair agencies have *less* power than they represent:

- You can dispute any inaccurate or incomplete information on your credit report, and the credit reporting agency (Equifax, Experian, and/or TransUnion) must investigate your dispute without charge to you. Therefore, everything a credit repair organization can do for you, you can do for yourself, at little to no cost.

- No one can legally remove accurate negative information from a credit report. Credit reporting agencies are obligated under the Fair Credit Reporting Act (FCRA) to correct or delete inaccurate, incomplete, or unverifiable information (usually within 30 days). They are not required to remove accurate information unless it is more than seven years old (or bankruptcies that are over 10 years old).

As we stated at the outset, we wrote this book for everyone. Being credit intelligent is an important way to save money, reduce risk, and improve your credit score.

There are non-profit credit counseling organizations that can help you develop a plan for managing your finances and improving your credit. For example, the National Foundation for Credit Counseling (NFCC) is a non-profit network that can refer you to a member in your area for credit counseling.

Smart Tips

You are credit smart when you:

- Seek assistance from proven professionals such as a consumer credit counselor to assist you in improving your credit score.
- Take responsibility for improving your credit score and don't look to credit repair agencies or any other companies that promise a quick change in your score.

In the next chapter, we will examine how debt-related stress can affect your health and provide some ideas on how you can minimize debt stress.

My Credit Intelligence Notes

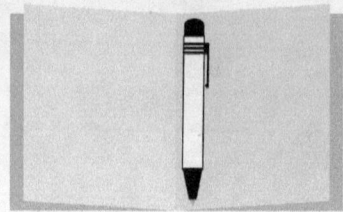

Chapter 8

Here's to Your Health:
Take Action to Avoid Debt Stress

Mava's kitchen. Weston, Connecticut.

Mava: *My shoulders and back are all knotted up with stress. They are killing me.*

Polly: *Why are you so worried?*

Mava: *This past year, it's been one storm after another, and we've had one expensive repair after another. None of this was expected or budgeted. And you know the way I am. Any kind of money stress always ends up knotting up my back, shoulders, and neck.*

Polly: *I can relate. The worry over my aunt's terminal illness and all those unexpected extra expenses has reactivated my ulcer.*

Close to 70 percent of Americans have a credit card, and the combined total of that outstanding debt exceeds $850 billion.[21] That's a lot of swiping, but not just at the mall, as you might expect. Nearly half of the households surveyed for the Demos 2012 "National Survey of Credit Card Debt of Low- and Middle- Income Households" have incurred credit debt because they used credit to pay for out-of-pocket medical expenses (such as prescriptions, co-pays, and deductibles) to afford treatment when funds were not readily available.[22] Nearly 40 percent of these families also charged basic living expenses (such as rent, utilities, and insurance) to make ends meet. The National Foundation for Credit Counseling (NFCC) "2014 Consumer Financial Literacy Survey" shows that roughly 35 percent of adults in the United States carry a balance from month to month on their credit cards. This is down 10 percent in the last five years, but 15 percent of adults still revolve a line of credit of $2,500 monthly.[23] All of this debt lingering over our heads causes what is known as "debt stress." The stress of debt affects each person's health differently. Some individuals suffer physically (30 percent), others experience mental health problems (33 percent), and many encounter both.[24] Knowing the signs of debt stress and living a proactive, healthy lifestyle will improve your ability to get out of debt while remaining in a positive frame of mind.

Who is Most Susceptible to Debt Stress?

The American Psychological Association's (APA) 2014 survey, *"Stress in America: Are Teens Adopting Adults' Stress Habits?"* revealed that money and work are reported as the highest stressors for approximately 70 percent of Americans.[25] The survey found that adults with children, women, and young adults bear the brunt of financial stress and subsequent health issues. The APA's 2015 survey, *"Stress in America: Paying With Our Health,"* reported that an alarming 54 percent of adults reported "they have 'just enough' or not enough money to make ends meet at the end of the month."[26] Evidence was also found that lack of funds restricts access to health care and a healthy lifestyle for these individuals and families. Furthermore, the 2015 APA survey documented that more than 50 percent of adults with high money stress were most likely to report sedentary means of coping such as watching television for more than two hours each day, surfing the Internet, napping, eating, drinking alcohol, and smoking. Sedentary coping measures such as these are contributing factors to unhealthy lifestyles.

With factors such as the lack of statutory sick pay for employees, job losses, and stagnated pay rates, keeping up with a tough economy and the ever-increasing cost of living is making Americans physically and mentally ill. A Gallup Poll found that individuals with student loans totaling more than $50,000 report a lesser sense of well-being in four areas (referred to in the poll as financial, physical, purpose, and community) in comparison to their debt-free counterparts.[27] The 2014 APA survey discovered the culture of stress in the United States is also impacting the health of 30-40 percent of teens, who reported symptoms such as irritability, anxiousness, and fatigue. This stress in teens was attributed to pressures other than debt.[28] Individuals who had positive coping mechanisms such as seeking emotional support, taking action towards a healthier lifestyle, and learning to better manage their finances reported considerably less stress and health problems in these surveys than those who did not have these habits.

How Debt Stress Impacts Health

Have you ever heard the phrase "worry yourself sick"? Recent research says it's a possibility. Illness can be caused by the body's physiological response to stress, which triggers the body's hormones into the fight-or-flight mode. This natural response causes both adrenaline and cortisol to begin to flow, which disturbs the day-to-day functions of other systems in our body. With persistent stress and continuous interruption of basic body functions, Mayo Clinic indicates that the body is "at increased risk of numerous health problems, including anxiety, depression, digestive problems, heart disease, sleep problems, weight gain, and memory and concentration impairment."[29] *Medical Daily* shared the results of analysis of the "Longitudinal Study of Adolescent Health," which found the physical effects of debt on young people (ages 24 to 32) with high debt to include, on average, a higher diastolic blood pressure by 1.3 percent.[30] Although this doesn't sound like much, a 2 percent increase in diastolic blood pressure is associated with a 17 percent increased risk of hypertension and a 15 percent increased risk for stroke.

The 2014 APA survey found that more than 30 percent of individuals in debt report eating too much or eating unhealthy foods as a result of debt stress.[31] Additionally, increased levels of cortisol associated with our body's natural fight or flight instinct are linked with the body to holding onto fat, carbohydrate cravings, and increased insulin production— all of which contribute to weight gain.[32] While stress does not cause digestive ailments, it is strongly associated with problems such as heartburn, irritable bowel syndrome, and ulcers.[33]

The research presented by *Medical Daily* also states that "people living with debt are three times more likely than others to suffer from mental illnesses, with depression symptoms worsening 14 percent for every 10 percent increase in personal debt."[34] When your thoughts are consumed with money matters, getting an adequate amount of sleep can seem impossible. Over 40 percent of adults participating in the 2014 APA survey reported insomnia as a result of high stress levels.[35] A literature review analyzing 65 prior studies was conducted by Dr. Thomas Richardson in 2013. His review found debt stressors to have a significant correlation with substance abuse problems and, in some cases, suicide.[36] Don't ignore your body and the physical and mental warning signs of debt stress. We suggest that you make positive coping mechanisms part of your daily routine.

How to Cope with Debt Stress

Dr. Kelly McGonigal, a health psychologist at Stanford University, stated that money and debt related stress is "one of the most toxic kinds of stress because it can't be compartmentalized."[37] When we feel stressed, positive coping measures can assist our bodies with releasing the debt stress. There are many methods of coping with and alleviating this stress, which permeates your mind and body. Just as the effects of stress cannot be compartmentalized, no single method will relieve all of the stress. Instead, you should seek a balance of coping mechanisms by implementing small steps of intentional effort to make positive changes in the areas of exercise, healthy eating, sleep, relaxation, emotional support, sensible budgeting, credit education, and paying down debt. It is possible for you to get relief from the burden of debt stress. Many individuals have successfully retrained their minds and bodies to help get their financial and physical health back on track.

Improve Your Health

It is easier to say "exercise and eat better" than it is to do so. You have to motivate yourself to take action, but you need to understand why it works before you're likely to get moving. HelpGuide.org[38] explains that exercise can act as a medication without any associated costs. The organization further explains that when you get enthusiastic and start purposeful exercise (walking, running, gardening, biking, stretching, swimming, and/or heavy-duty house cleaning), the physical discomfort you have been feeling begins to disappear. (You should seek advice from a physician before you undertake a new exercise regimen.) With physical activity, your brain releases endorphins that relax your muscles, alleviate tension within the body, and help migraine headaches diminish. As your body relaxes, your mind follows suit. Are you motivated yet?

Practice clean eating to maximize your new healthy lifestyle. Avoid processed foods and eliminate fast food from your diet. Fruits and vegetables can be expensive at the grocery store. Spend one weekend morning doing price comparisons at the local farmer's market and produce stands. You'll find your favorite fresh foods are less expensive at local markets/ stands and fresher than their grocery store counterparts. Prepare more food at dinner than you or your family will eat. After dinner, package leftovers for each person in the family to take for lunch the following day. To avoid the pitfalls of a growling tummy while passing by a tempting fast food restaurant, keep healthy, ready-to-eat snacks in your purse or car. You can make excuses all day that processed and fast foods are cheaper than eating healthy, but with a little extra effort each week, you can begin to cut these bad habits out of your life.

Relaxation isn't a Luxury

To round out your new healthy lifestyle, you must pay attention to the health of your mind. Stress caused by money issues has been reported to cause irritability, anxiousness, discouragement, exhaustion, and sadness.[39] Regaining control over your body's reaction to stress should include a concerted effort to ease these conditions. The connection between depression and debt stress is well documented,[40] so you must maintain hope and take proactive steps to relieve these symptoms. While seeking emotional support from a trusted friend or family member is ideal,[41] you may not be comfortable with opening up about this painful experience. Many people choose to speak with a mental health counselor about their money woes. This may not be feasible for you if you don't have health insurance coverage or the funds for office visit co-pays.

Other techniques which are free and have shown significant impact on levels of stress are deep breathing exercises, progressive muscle relaxation, meditation, and visualization.[42] Try listening to music for relaxation and distraction from stress, as it is effective for reducing both physical and physiological symptoms of stress.[43] Debt stress enters the body through your mind. You have the power to regain emotional health by purging constant negative thoughts and replacing them with positive ones. Spending quality time around loved ones is also good for you. Believe in yourself and your ability to cope with financial stress in a proactive way, and you will achieve your goal.

Document Your Monthly Budget

According to a Gallup Poll conducted in 2013, over 65 percent of American's don't have a budget.[44] The French writer and aviator Antoine de Saint-Exupery said it best, "A goal without a plan is just a wish." That advice rings true in so many aspects of our lives, but it is especially true when it comes to finances. You will not end the cycle of debt stress that destroys your physical and emotional well-being until you sit down to document your expenses and your income. Let's go step-by-step and do this together.

1. Pull out copies of all of your bills and sit down with a calculator, a pen, and a piece of paper. If you want to follow a budget worksheet to help you document your expenses, many can be found online.
2. Write out all fixed expenses. Fixed expenses are typically the exact same amount each and every month. They include items such as rent/mortgage payments, utility bills, insurance premiums, and car payments. If the bill is the exact same amount every month, it is a fixed expense. Don't forget to include your income taxes.
3. Next, you will document a typical month's variable expenses. Like it sounds, variable expenses change slightly from month to month. Examples of variable expenses include groceries, gasoline, drinks out with friends, meals at restaurants and/or take-out, clothing, and entertainment. It is essential to include the minor expenses you incur on a daily and weekly basis, as they add up quickly.
4. Calculate your total monthly expenses by first adding your monthly fixed expenses. Next, add the variable expenses for the month together. Any purchases made on a daily or weekly basis should be calculated into monthly totals and added to the total variable expenses. Finally, add the fixed and variable expenses together and you will know your total monthly expenses.
5. Knowing how much money is coming into your household each month is equally as important to the budgeting process. Calculate how much money you earn each month.

Now it's time to be honest with yourself. Are you spending more than you make? Does it look like there should be money left over each month, but you're still living paycheck to paycheck? It's time to identify means of earning more money or to cut your actual expenses. You could get stuck here and continue to let money stress you out, or you can do something about it. It is your choice.

Take Control of Your Finances

By knowing where your hard-earned dollars go each and every month, you can take control of your finances. Find a budget that works for you and stick with it, as we discuss in the next chapter.

Face Current Debt Head-on

Avoidance may seem like the easy way to avoid debt stress. As we discussed earlier, this seriously impacts your physical and mental health. Use the following guidance, and you can make serious progress towards ending the cycle of debt in your life. Remember, better financial health paves the way to increased health and overall well-being. We recommend that you take these steps to deal with your debt:

1. Start by opening your mail and organizing your bills based on due date and collection status.
2. Contact the creditors of bills that have not been sent to collections yet. Explain that your financial situation was caused by a hardship, and you wish to set up a payment plan to take care of your debt. Because you have assessed your budget, you will know how much you can afford to pay and how frequently.
3. Pay the agreed upon amount, on or before the due date you agreed to. If you do not abide by these payment arrangements, it is likely the creditor will send the account directly into collections.

By paying on debt before it goes to a collection agency, you have taken a critical step in preventing more unpaid debt and negative items being added to your credit report. Taking responsibility for unpaid bills now stops your credit score from continuing to decline.

Don't Hide from Debt Collectors

Once you have paid down the bills that have not yet gone to debt collections, you are ready to begin making payment arrangements on the accounts already showing on your credit report. Many books, websites, and resources exist on how to repair your credit. Please familiarize yourself with those resources and take action. To reduce the debt stress caused when accepting collection agency calls, we encourage you to learn your rights as a consumer and learn how to communicate with debt collectors. The following information should be helpful when you deal with debt collectors:

- Request free copies of your credit report from all three credit bureaus. Credit reporting is not uniform and is considered voluntary, so you cannot assume all of the reports will have the same data.[45] This topic is discussed in Chapter 6.
- Equally important as obtaining your credit report is learning how to read your credit report. The online resources for this are also plentiful. If you're a hands-on kind of person, you may want to take copies of your reports into your bank and ask for help deciphering what each line item means. Polly provides additional information on credit reports and their components in her book, *The Plastic Effect*.[46]
- Dispute errors on your credit report immediately. Follow the instructions each bureau provides on their website exactly. Along with completed dispute forms, write your own dispute letter detailing why the information is incorrect. Include supporting documentation with your dispute form and letter. Send correspondence with tracking numbers to document delivery and acceptance. The bureaus must reply within 30 days. Keep precise records of all communications sent and received to protect yourself.
- Understand the statute of limitations on debt to avoid instances of zombie debt. As Polly stated in an article in the *Arizona Independent Daily*,[47] "Zombie debt occurs

when a collection agency tries to resurrect credit card debt that is time-barred or has already been paid in full." There is also a detailed discussion of zombie debt in *The Plastic Effect.*[48]

- If you are only able to make payments on one account at a time, answer the phone when any creditor calls and let them know you are making an effort to pay down debts. Give them a reasonable time frame to contact you back about resolving the debt owed to their agency. Keep track on your calendar which accounts you plan to pay back next and who you are dealing with at the corresponding collection agency.
- Set up payment plans you can honor. If something happens that is going to prohibit an on-time payment, be proactive and reach out to the representative handling your account to renegotiate your payment schedule.

So, what next? Take personal responsibility for your debt. Commit to educating yourself on managing and paying down your debt. Understand you are not alone in your financial woes. Recognize the larger picture of economic recovery going on in our country. Use the practical tools we have suggested for coping with the mental and physical toll that debt stress plays on your body. Financial hardship is not the end of your world. Be credit smart both in the future and today by being actively engaged in resolving your budgetary and debt stressors.

Smart Tips

You are credit smart when you:

- Are aware of which physical symptoms relate to your credit card debt.
- Use positive coping mechanisms for dealing with stress.
- Take control of your money, instead of letting your money control you.
- Reach out for assistance to help alleviate stress and anxiety you may be feeling related to your credit card debt.

In the next chapter, we will discuss how debt can affect your relationships. We will also offer some credit intelligent ways to communicate about your finances that may improve the health of your relationship.

My Credit Intelligence Notes

Chapter 9

Debt Can Kill Romance:
Credit Problems Can Create Havoc
in All of Your Relationships

Lunch, after shopping all morning, Palazzo Hotel. Las Vegas, Nevada.

Polly: *Oh, my gosh! I can't believe I forgot to tell you who's getting a divorce.*

Mava: *Spill it.*

Polly: *Mr. Perfect. Sam from the credit card industry—who had the perfect marriage, the perfect house, and the perfect second house. He got laid off and nearly ended up filing for bankruptcy.*

Mava: *You've got to be kidding!*

Polly: *And there's more! He found out that his wife had built up and was hiding thousands of dollars of credit card debt that he never knew about, and that, alone, made matters even worse. That was the final straw.*

Mava: *I'm all ears. Keep going.*

Polly: *So anyways. It's unclear whether he left her, or she left him, but the whole marriage exploded and the credit card debt is all on the table for the lawyers to figure out.*

Mava: *What a mess! It sounds like they might have stayed together were it not for the hidden credit card debt.*

There is a prevalent problem in our society today related to credit and how it's breaking up relationships. It's certainly something that we've noticed has been escalating during the 25+ years of our friendship. So many of the people we know and have come into contact with have struggled with their relationships as a result of money and credit issues.

This doesn't surprise us, because the economy is at the worst point that most people have experienced in their lifetimes. We know people who can't put their children through college, and others who have lost their jobs, their homes, and have gone through their savings. This is an unprecedented time. Making a relationship work is difficult enough. Add financial stress on top of it, and you have a powder keg.

It's no wonder that stress over issues of credit and money can cause problems of trust, power struggles, fear, and more.

During the writing of this book, we became even more aware of how critical it is to be credit smart, because money and credit are possibly the most important influences in a person's life today. This is because financial matters have such a strong influence on health, emotions, relationships, identity, and therefore, your future. We believe that people involved in a credit intelligent relationship have a better chance of making it these days.

We've heard about and witnessed so many ways that people make purchases and then creatively hide, camouflage, or explain away the evidence to their better half. These include:

- Using the classic response of "this old thing" (when asked about a new purchase).
- Keeping new purchases in the trunk of the car or hiding them in the garage until "the coast is clear" to bring them inside.
- Saying the item belongs to a friend and that either it's borrowed or it was given to them (for example, this dress didn't fit my friend so she gave it to me).
- Bringing items into the house when your partner is sleeping or too caught up watching a favorite television show to notice.
- Hiding a new purchase in a closet or under the bed and then, during a sudden episode of needing to tidy up, the "old" item is conveniently "rediscovered."

The list really does go on and on.

Have you used any of the above, or do you have a few methods of your own that you use to disguise purchases from your significant other?

Here are some additional credit and money issues that we have observed and that we have seen play havoc with relationships:

- differences in money management styles
- one person worries more about your money than the other
- one or both partners have a penchant for expensive things that the budget can't afford
- the investment priorities of each person are not the same
- one or both incomes are not stable
- one person is a saver and the other is a spender
- there's a power struggle for who's in charge of how money will be spent—i.e., does the person who makes the most money feel they deserve the most decision-making power?

- each person has different values associated with how to spend money—e.g., one wants to buy clothes at Target and the other wants to go to Macy's
- one is willing to take financial risks more than the other—e.g., certain investments, gambling, get-rich-quick schemes, etc.
- disagreement about merging finances

Part of being credit intelligent includes knowing there may be a better way! In doing so, you can also:

- Decrease the anxiety associated with that feeling of being "found out,"
- Decrease the guilt you feel when you're hiding something,
- Increase the chance of keeping joint finances on more solid footing, and
- Increase the chance of supporting the healthy financial aspects of your relationship and, therefore, supporting your overall relationship.

As with many things in life, success with finances requires a certain amount of discipline and commitment. Setting out a game plan ahead of time can pave the way and make the process smoother. The following are a few ideas and some food for thought that you may find useful, but the approach you ultimately find best for you may end up being as unique as you are. As a couple, you should:

- **Decide together how often you want to sit down to discuss your finances.** Do you want to schedule regular meetings on the calendar? Or wait until emergencies strike?
- **Commit to jointly assessing and addressing your credit scores.** Do you want to set goals for raising one or both of your scores? Or do you simply want to monitor your scores for accuracy?
- **Discuss how you want to approach obtaining credit.** Do you want your accounts to always be in both your names together? Always in your separate names? A combination of joint and separate accounts? There can

be a benefit to having credit in your separate names because, as joint account holders, mismanagement on the part of either party will damage the credit of both parties. This is because credit reports are for specific individuals, not couples. Both positive and negative information on a joint account is reported to the credit agencies for each person's individual credit report.

- **Talk about budgeting and spending limits.** Do you each have a weekly budget that you are free to spend on whatever you want without consulting the other? If so, what's that amount? What's the dollar amount that's the tipping point beyond which one of you will feel unfairly considered, maybe even bitter, if not consulted first? What can you afford to spend on unplanned items?

- **Anticipate major money commitments with major budget planning and discussion.** If and when you plan for one of life's significant expenditures (such as a vacation, car, or house; and perhaps even retirement or the care of a loved one), emotions of excitement and stress can begin to intermingle with the decisions being made, including the decisions regarding credit. Careful and thoughtful budget planning and discussion done together in advance of this type of expenditure will go a long way towards helping you to chart a course toward a successful outcome.

- **Agree with your partner to "walk in the shoes of the other."** Year after year, in the results of multiple surveys, marriage counselors report that the number one issue that couples argue about most is money. Think about this: if you and your partner practiced the five tips outlined above and didn't commit a breach in your financial agreement and then agreed to "walk in the shoes of the other" (i.e., view your spending and credit behavior from the vantage point of the other) **do you think you would have a fresh, credit intelligent start?**

Let's talk for a minute about the association between money and relationships. Without money issues, marriage counselors and relationship surveys—and tabloid publications, for that matter—would have a whole lot less to talk about. There has been a consistent theme in the storylines of the troubled, and there is a common bond linking the struggles in the relationships of couples across all walks of life, whether rich or poor. Specifically, couples argue about money more frequently than anything else.

The stakes are high, because virtually every thread of the fabric woven throughout our lives is touched and affected by money in some way. The following list provides a few examples and ideas to get you thinking. As you review this list, reflect on the vast scope of circumstances and questions to be considered by you and your partner relative to money. It's easy to understand how and why money is such a commonly fought about item amongst couples—whether they have it or not. Important topics to consider include:

- Are you saving for retirement? How?
- Is secret spending or little white lies about items purchased harpooning mutual trust?
- Do you need to financially accommodate aging parents? Do you agree?
- How many purchases should you make on credit (and which ones) versus pay by cash (or another form of payment)?
- Are your money "talks" ending up as hurtful arguments, like those of many people?
- How are you going to support and educate your children?
- How do you want to invest? Where and how much?
- Are you totally avoiding talking about money, like most people?

Being money smart—and credit intelligent—can also be a way to be kind to yourself and your relationship.

Knowledge is power. Your relationship is important to you. If any of the pitfalls we discussed sound familiar, think about how the following smart tips might be helpful to you.

Smart Tips

You are credit smart when you:

- Learn about money management skills as a couple. This could include buying a book, ordering an audio course, or attending a seminar.
- Make a financial plan together.
- Create a bookkeeping system to track your expenses that works for both of you.
- Discuss your finances and expenses openly with your partner. Silence is not golden.
- Make new vows together to change your relationship with money.
- Determine spending limits together. This means that neither of you spends more than the maximum agreed amount without prior discussion and agreement between the two of you.

We will examine two more key components of credit intelligence in the next chapter—understanding how to protect your identity to help prevent identity theft and fraud, and knowing how to navigate the perils associated with online shopping.

My Credit Intelligence Notes

Chapter 10

The New Status Quo:
Protecting Your Identity and
Avoiding Online Shopping Perils

Verizon Phone Store. Los Angeles, California.

Mava: *Polly, I am so incredibly embarrassed. My credit card was just declined.*

Polly: *You have got to be kidding. With your credit limit, you got declined?*

Mava: *It's not about my credit limit. I forgot to call the bank to say I was traveling out of state, and they thought this purchase was fraud, so they declined me. I had to use another card. As soon we get out of here, I'll call the bank.*

Polly: *I hear this story all the time. Since consumers no longer have liability for credit card fraud, banks have had to put steps in place to tighten security measures.*

To navigate down today's new credit superhighway and be in step with today's new credit card status quo, you need to be aware of a number of things. These include the way you shop, the new payment methods and tools available, revised bank policies, increased bank security for fraud protection and detection, and more.

In the example above, if Mava would have called her bank in advance and advised them of her travel, she would have avoided the embarrassment of being declined at the point-of-sale.

Also, as part of this new status quo, banks have a tendency to decline more sales on credit cards. This is due to a number of factors such as increased delinquencies, fraud, and over-limit transactions. The decline rate varies by bank and by type of card.

As we stated, fraud is one of the factors that has resulted in banks needing to tighten up their security measures. Credit card fraud has also driven up the cost of transactions and has resulted in cardholders needing to take additional precautions to be credit intelligent.

Overviews of how your identity can be stolen and how you can help prevent identity theft from occurring can be found in articles from The National Crime Prevention Council,[49] TransUnion,[50] and in many other articles, blogs, and industry advisories. Many tips you've heard before, while many others are common sense.

To be credit intelligent, you need to be aware of key areas where your identity is vulnerable.

Perhaps one of the most important things you can do is to be aware of key vulnerabilities and then consistently follow through with key steps to protect yourself in these areas. These steps may seem basic, but they are credit intelligent. Taking these precautions can go a long way in helping secure your credit identity. The following areas should be addressed to help protect your identity:

- **Your Social Security number:** Let's start by talking about a major source of identity theft: Social Security numbers. This is the source of a lot of wrong-doing that results in a significant amount of credit card theft. Your Social Security number is all an identity thief needs to commit an easy crime. This type of crime against you is not only anguishing on many levels, but creates upheaval in your life and consumes untold amounts of your time in order to set right. Therefore, in all ways and in all forms, guard your Social Security number like it is your life—because in many ways it is. Ways to protect your Social Security number include:
  - Never print your social security number or have it printed on materials that will be seen by the public or multiple people, such as on your personal bank checks.
  - As a rule, you should never give out your Social Security number anyone over the phone—unless you know them exceedingly well on a personal basis, like a family member. It is extremely important to understand that institutions like banks and the IRS will *never* ask for your Social Security number over the phone.
  - Only provide your Social Security number to trusted sources when it is needed and when you know it is secure.
  - Never throw anything out in the garbage can that contains or has your Social Security number printed on it.
- **Your mailbox and your garbage can:** Next, let's talk about a couple of gold mines for identity thieves: what goes into your garbage can and your mailbox. Seriously! Mailboxes and garbage cans are playgrounds of opportunity containing massive quantities of material and data for an identity thief to capitalize on. Let's break it down and look at some examples and some solutions. These may seem obvious, but again, it's often a matter of staying aware and diligent:

- A mailbox that is curbside is easy pickings for an identify thief. It makes it easy for someone to grab the mail you've left for the postal carrier or the mail the postal carrier has left in the mailbox for you. With all that information in hand, an identify thief can create havoc with your life.

- Examples of information found inside mailboxes and garbage that identity thieves can derive or leverage value from include your credit card payments, information on bank loans, bank and credit card statements, all those pre-approved credit card offers (they can fill them out in your name and have them sent to their address), checks you've written, and countless other types of documents with important information.

- While solutions may seem straightforward and simple, they do require some diligence and discipline, and perhaps a few dollars to implement. Examples include:
  - Always shred or tear into tiny pieces any pre-approved credit card offer, bank and credit card statements, your phone bill, anything with your Social Security number on it, etc.
  - Consider investing in a small home shredder for this purpose.
  - Consider installing a lockable mailbox.

- **Additional vulnerabilities for identity theft:** From hacking into computers to steal personal data to filing a change of address form in a victim's name to divert their mail and obtain their personal and financial data, identity thieves appear tireless and clever. You can be your best ally and advocate by being aware of a few additional vulnerabilities. You must be consistently vigilant and mindful of the solutions and follow through to protect your identity. Examples include:
  - **Passwords.** We all have a lot of them. Make sure they are difficult to figure out. Use a combination of upper and lower case letters, numbers, and symbols to create strong passwords. Do not use the

same password for all of your accounts. Memorize them. Put them in a secure location at home or in a safe deposit box. Register them with an online encryption service. But do not carry them with you.

- **Wallets and purses.** We all have them. Limit the amount of sensitive information you carry in them. In case your wallet or purse becomes lost or stolen, have a separate list of all your credit cards and bank cards which you have prepared in advance and keep stored in a safe place. Use this list to quickly call the card issuers to inform them. Your list should include your account numbers, expiration dates, and the customer service and fraud department telephone numbers of the issuing bank.[51]

- **Online transactions.** Most of us make them. You should be aware of the ways that online transactions expose you to a number of potential vulnerabilities for identity theft. Here are some tips to reduce your exposure to these vulnerabilities.

  o If possible, pay for online purchases directly with a credit card (instead of a check). This also provides you with the benefit of being able to dispute the charge if it happens that your item(s) doesn't arrive or was not as represented.

  o Polly and Mava prefer to use only one specific credit card for online shopping. It makes it easier to monitor that one credit card closely for online fraud. It also makes it easier to monitor other credit cards for fraud because we know there should not be any online purchases showing up on the statements of our other credit cards.

  o When making online transactions, it's necessary for you to enter your credit card information and other personal information. How can you help protect yourself from credit thieves, scams like phishing, and websites that are fraudulent? Here's how (and like we promised at the beginning of this book, we're not going to start talking technical and get all complicated). One simple way to protect yourself is to go to the top of your computer screen and look at a website's address in the browser. You want the beginning of the address to say "https" instead of "http". The addition of the "s" means that the website has been secured using an SSL Certificate; the "s" stands for "secure." There are different levels of security on websites. Websites that have the highest level of security available will also have a little "lock" icon in the same area as the website address. The little lock is not just a picture—you can click on it and see details of the website's security.

o   Here are a few additional credit intelligent steps for online transactions that may seem to be common sense, but require a bit of time and effort. Look for signs as to whether an online merchant is real or if it is a hoax which could lead to identity or credit theft. Look at the website carefully before making a purchase. Check the website address in your browser to make sure you were not redirected to a fake website that mimics a well-known site (clicking on links for a site instead of typing in the website's address can cause this to happen). Also, be aware that reputable sites and companies generally have several hallmarks including a listed physical address and phone number, a return policy, and a privacy statement.

o   Mava and Polly offer an additional word of caution about websites that offer prices that are too low to be believed, prizes, or giveaways. This relates to personal experience as well as to information that we've gleaned from research. This advice can be summarized in the adages "if it seems too good to be true, then it probably is" and "nothing is really free." The prize or giveaway is almost always related to the merchant wanting something from you—if not more money, then more of your personal information.

- **Stay tight and current.**
  - ○ Maintaining an older line of credit or, in other words, older credit cards, can have the benefit of positively affecting your credit score. On the other hand, hanging on to credit cards for inactive accounts and the billing materials that accompany them can also present additional opportunities for identity thieves. Therefore, carefully consider which credit cards you want to use and keep. Consider canceling any newer, inactive credit card accounts so that they can't be abused by identity thieves.
  - ○ Limit the number of credit cards you have, so that you can ensure you have an active handle on them at all times. By that, we mean make sure that you are reconciling your credit card statements regularly. Make sure that you question and challenge any purchases you did not make. Call your credit card issuer and let them know if you find any errors or fraudulent charges. You should be taking this same step with your bank statement, utility bills, and other bills, too, to make sure that all the charges shown are actually yours.
  - ○ Did you close a checking account? If so, did you destroy all the checks? You should do so immediately upon closing the account. Keep any checks for your current account in a safe place. Do not have the bank send any new checks to your home address. Instead, pick them up from the bank. Look through your new order of checks to make sure it is complete

and no checks are missing. Alert your bank immediately if there is a problem with the check order.

o Check your credit report regularly to make sure no accounts are reported that you didn't authorize. Contact the issuing bank and the credit bureau immediately if you find this type of fraud.

Don't be scammed over the phone by anyone wanting your credit card number or Social Security number. Whenever anyone calls you on the phone, you never really know who's on the other end. There are a number of legitimate institutions and businesses (such as banks and the IRS) who will *never* contact you by phone and who would *never* ask you to give your Social Security number or credit card number over the phone. If you get a call asking for this information, no matter how urgent it sounds, it's very likely fraud. These calls could take many forms and could range from credit repair scams to fake IRS calls. If you feel a call is questionable, you can always call your bank or credit card company using a phone number that is listed on your statement to inquire about the issue and make sure it is legitimate.

Don't be afraid to call your credit card company. With fraud being so prevalent, call your credit card company and let them know when you're doing any of the following:

- Making a higher purchase than normal,
- Using your card more frequently than normal,
- Traveling some place out of your area, such as out of state,
- Changing your shopping patterns, or
- Making a significant purchase that falls outside of your normal shopping history.

Fraud can occur when you're making purchases close to home, while traveling, or when shopping online. For some, however, it seems that online payment options increase

**temptation and make it even easier to spend more money.
Shopping online has its own set of fraud and spending perils.**

Like many people, Mava works all day, every day. Most of her shopping is done at night (often in the middle of the night) on her computer, while sitting in bed. And many times, when she's too tired to be shopping, she gets carried away and spends too much. When all it takes is a few clicks of the mouse, buying and spending money is all too easy.

But guess who also spends too much by shopping online? Polly! Polly is inspired to shop online for her grandchildren, who live across the country, because she can take advantage of convenient wish list shopping, gift wrap, and direct shipping. She sends just about everything under the sun because "it's on the grandchildren's wish list and I was sent an alert."

Maybe you've discovered, too, that online shopping opportunities are endless, and that they beckon you to buy, and buy more, and at the end of the month your credit card balance increases as a result.

We are not alone!

This is confirmed by many blogs and articles that we found through our extensive research for this book. The perils of online shopping are part of the new status quo.

The bottom line is that there are lots of temptations and dangers in the online shopping world! Certainly, it can be a hazard to your credit health. Online retailers are savvy, and they know how to get you to spend, spend, spend again, and then spend more.

The longer you research and shop, the more you are likely to spend.

Want to try browsing around shopping sites on the Internet just for fun? Browsing is great. Registering your credit card information and shopping is a different matter. This can be dangerous territory!

If you think online shopping is safer, less tempting, or more credit intelligent than going to a brick-and-mortar retailer, think again! The following list includes only a few of the tricks, ploys, and requests that online retailers use "for your convenience" in order to get you to spend more money with them and to return and spend more money. A few of the items on the list are common things that we do to ourselves!

When shopping online, proceed with caution before doing any of the following, because these habits and activities can cause you to spend more money than you had planned and, therefore, can create potential credit issues.

This is a partial and limited list of favorite "cautions" we've pulled together after talking to many friends and associates and through our personal experiences. After sorting through hundreds of stories that have similar themes, storylines, and buyer's remorse "I can't believe it happened to me" endings, these are our top picks to share with you:

Danger! Registering your credit card on a retail website. This makes it exceedingly easy for you to spend and spend some more, time and again. It also allows the website to track your spending and then offer you more daily spending opportunities. If the online retailer experiences a security breach, your nightmare has just begun.

Danger! One click "Buy Now" button. This allows you to buy items even faster—perhaps too fast?

Danger! "Those who bought that also bought this."

Danger! The little clock/timer in the corner that counts down the minutes before the time is up and the item disappears from your shopping cart. This forces you to buy fast and may not allow enough time to consider the purchase.

Danger! Bookmarking shopping sites. This allows you to access them on a whim and impulse—perhaps too quickly and easily?

Danger! Online retailers track your purchases and the items you look at. Then they offer deals and additional items you may want to see as you shop the site and when you check-out.

Danger! Online shopping that's done in a hurry, and perhaps without enough time to think, reflect, and consider all options, needs, desires, budget, etc.

Danger! Online shopping that is done while drinking an alcoholic beverage, eating, and/or being distracted.

These activities can all result in making online shopping decisions that are less than optimal.

Bottom line: You can spend a ton of money in minutes when you never meant to, have buyer's remorse, or not have the item you really wanted. Can you return it? Yes. But, will you? That's a different question. And if you do, then that takes additional time and, sometimes, additional money as well.

What's the credit intelligent approach to online shopping?

As with so many things in life, the answer is often "Think!"

Simply do the *opposite* of all of the above!

For example, do *not*:

- Set up one-click buying.
- Bookmark online retail buying sites.
- Give in to the little ticking clock or timer in the corner.
- Buy the special "add-on" product at the end of your purchase.

Beware of recurring payments and auto-ship. Many organizations try to get you to sign up for this. There are many reasons you should think twice before you make this move, including a decrease in customer service that has made it more difficult to cancel your decision once it's made.

Check your current credit card statements to see what you are currently being charged for and paying on a recurring basis. Determine if you want to continue to receive and pay for these ongoing products and services. Some of the recurring payments and services that many people want to receive range from home oil delivery to magazines, from utilities to medicine prescription refills. There are many other such credit card charges, however, that people have either erroneously signed up for or have long forgotten about, and they are losing money each month by not canceling them. If you want to discontinue any products or services, contact each of the companies according to their directions (usually either by phone or in writing) and register your request. If you do not receive a satisfactory response and they do not comply with your request, then contact your credit card company for assistance in canceling the transaction.

Smart Tips

You are credit smart when you:

- Are mindful of identity fraud and how to protect yourself.
- Communicate to your card company if you plan to travel or if you are going to make a large or out-of-pattern credit card purchase.
- Shred all pre-approved credit card applications.
- Protect your Social Security number.
- Understand what recurring payments and auto-ship purchases are.
- Set limits around your online shopping.

In the next chapter, we will introduce you to Chip & PIN cards and explain the benefits of this technology. We will also explain the differences between Chip & PIN cards and traditional credit cards, including changes in how transactions are made using these cards.

My Credit Intelligence Notes

Chapter 11

New Cards:
Chip & PIN Cards Are Here to Stay

Hotel in Austin, Texas.

Mava: *Sorry, but I just had to call you first thing this morning to tell you what I just found out. You won't believe what happened with my brand new credit card! I woke up to warning emails and texts from the fraud department of my bank.*

Polly: *Didn't your bank just replace your cards with a new Chip & PIN card a couple of weeks ago? And now you're saying it will need to be replaced again?*

Mava: *That's right! There was already attempted fraud on my new Chip & PIN card, but because of the security this type of card provides, the bank was able to detect it right away and verify the fraud with me. We were able to cancel the card and a new one will be in my hands soon.*

Polly: *According to the industry conferences I've been attending, the number of occurrences of counterfeit card fraud in the United States is expected to decrease by 80-90 percent, because Chip & PIN cards can't be duplicated.*

Mava: *The bank told me that that's exactly the way they were able to detect the fraud on my card—because someone attempted to duplicate the card and failed.*

With all of the data breaches at major retailers in the United States, consumer demand for more secure transactions is at an all-time high. A solution has been in the works for over a decade through a collaborative effort between Europay, MasterCard & Visa (EMV). This technology authenticates physical cards at ATMs and point-of-sale (POS) terminals. Starting in the fourth quarter of 2014, financial institutions began issuing cardholders new credit cards that contained this new solution to replace their current credit cards. Additionally, merchants began replacing their terminals to accommodate this new technology.

Whereas global implementation started in 2005, the US roll-out of EMV card acceptance began in retail stores in October 2014 and will finish with gas pumps in 2017. This change is mandated by the card associations. What's this mean for you? Expect cards to look different, POS terminals to require more input from you the customer, and fraud rates resulting from face-to-face transactions to decline.

Retail stores and other card-present environments must adapt to the new equipment requirements and payment procedures or face liability from future fraud losses. Unfortunately, using a Chip & PIN card for online payments and other online purchases still has just as much risk as using a non-Chip & PIN credit card.

Don't worry! Until all new terminals are installed at the end of 2017, the new Chip & PIN cards can be used at existing terminals.

While EMV sounds new, it is a patented technology with over four decades of research into best practices and security.

Without getting to into a lot of tech-speak, EMV is a global standard for security and compatibility of smart cards across all payment networks. The actual cards using the EMV standard are referred to across the world as Chip & PIN cards. The Chip technology was patented in the 1970s.[52]

One of the first widespread uses of EMV technology was when universities adopted smart cards as an all-in-one card that functions as a student ID, a cash card for on-campus expenses, and an ATM card for student bank accounts. These cards are now used by hundreds of millions of college students globally[53] at the merchants in university communities.

You'll be able to look at your credit cards and tell the difference between Chip & PIN cards and their less secure counterparts.

Here in the United States, cardholders have started to receive new Chip & PIN cards in the mail, despite expiration dates of their existing cards being years away. You'll know you've received a Chip & PIN card by the rectangular gold microprocessor on the face. This computer chip on the card protects your data during a transaction at any store you physically visit to make a purchase. You'll see what looks like tiny wires on the gold computer chip. Those wires serve as electrical contact points when the card is inserted into the ATM or POS terminal. These contact points create a secure transaction that crooks can't replicate in skimming scams and the like. The transaction occurs between the contact points within the card and the contact points in the terminal, instead of the terminal reading the magnetic strip on the back of the card.

While more secure, Chip & PIN cards require more consumer participation at the terminal.

Are you already fatigued by choosing the payment type, verifying the transaction amount, typing in a PIN, and remembering to press the enter button at a payment terminal? If the answer is yes, you may need to practice some relaxation exercises when Chip & PIN terminals launch at your favorite store. All improvements in life come with a learning curve, and increased security at the register comes with a price to our patience. Instead of swiping the card to start the payment, you will insert the credit card in the terminal and leave it until the end of the transaction. This step bears repeating. *Insert the smart card and leave it.*

Whether you realize it or not, you've already been in training for the next few steps of an EMV transaction. Answer all of the transaction-related questions as they appear on the screen, as you have been doing for the last few years.

Memorize, protect, and randomize your PINs for added security.

What comes next may be perplexing, but is essential for the security of these cards. The name "Chip & PIN" or, as some people call them, "Chip & Signature" cards comes from the next step of the transaction. Until now, your signature has been the standard for credit card transactions. Now a PIN may also be required. This is worth repeating. *Be prepared to sign and to also enter a PIN, even if you're using a credit card.* But be aware that you won't always be asked for a PIN. For your new EMV card, we recommend increasing the length of your PIN to six digits to boost password strength. Make sure to contact your issuing bank to confirm it is time to shred your old card (without the chip) once the EMV card arrives.

Create personal reminder cues to remember to pull the Chip & PIN card out of the terminal at the end of transaction.

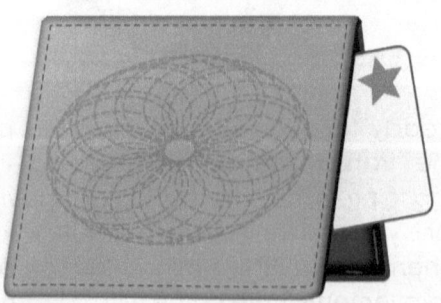

Once a transaction is completed, *remove your Chip & PIN card from the POS terminal.* That's right, you will have to remember to retrieve your card and put it back in your wallet at the *end* of the transaction. This habit takes some getting used to. Signs posted by retailers will remind you to retrieve the EMV card from the terminal and put your plastic away after the payment is finished. You'll also want to develop some of your own personal cues to assist you with making card retrieval a routine step in your purchases. Polly and Mava always leave their wallets out until the end of the transaction, when they put their cards back in their wallets. This little reminder will keep you from getting all the way to the car, only to remember that you left your card at the checkout. All the technology in the world will not replace you taking personal responsibility for the physical security of your card.

Smart Tips

You are credit smart when you:

- Take the time to educate yourself on the advantages of the new Chip & PIN cards being issued.
- Make purchases using the Chip & PIN card, which gives you additional levels of security.
- Verify with your issuing bank that your Chip & PIN card can be easily utilized in the locations where you are traveling.
- Realize that all new payment programs have a learning curve.
- Check with your issuing bank for directions on when to shred your non-EMV cards.
- Activate the new cards and sign the signature panel as soon as they are received.
- Understand that PIN numbers will increase to 6 digits and that you should not use dates such as anniversaries and birthdays as your PIN.
- Understand that physical security remains your responsibility. Be sure to remove your card from the point-of-sale terminal at the end of transaction. Do *not* write your PIN number on your card.
- Pay attention to the instructions if you are using an ATM located outside of the United States. These instructions remind you to remove your card from the machine, because international ATMs do not automatically return to the card to you at the end of the transaction.

- Upon receiving your new Chip & PIN card in the mail, check for a new expiration date and/or possibly a new card number and communicate the new card data to any companies with whom you have set up automatic payments.
- Expect to see changes in the physical appearance of the plastic. Some issuers are no longer using raised, embossed numbers and letters.

My Credit Intelligence Notes

Chapter 12

A Roadmap to Credit Intelligence:
All 85 Smart Tips at Your Fingertips

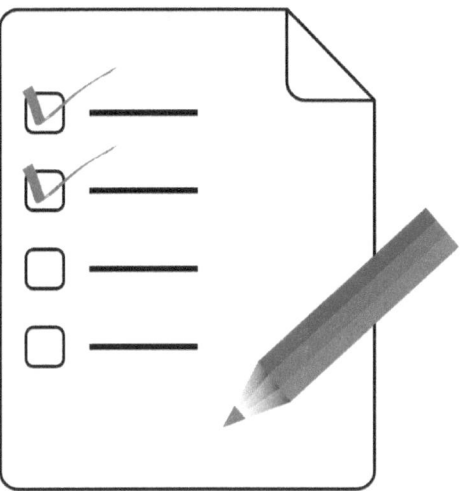

In order to further help increase your credit intelligence, this chapter provides a compilation of all the smart tips from all of the chapters of this book. We recommend that you go through this list of smart tips and check them off.

Thank you for taking this journey with us. We wish you a prosperous, healthy, credit intelligent life.

Introduction: What Does "Credit Smart" Mean?

You are credit smart when you:

- ✓ Pay your balances in full, to avoid paying interest.
- ✓ Selectively use your credit card for daily living expenses, to most effectively live within your budget.
- ✓ Are aware of your credit score and its accuracy, to maintain your purchasing power.
- ✓ Limit the number of credit cards you have and use, to help control your credit score.
- ✓ Make your credit card payments on time, to avoid late fees and negative entries on your credit reports.
- ✓ Never take cash advances on a credit card, to avoid one of the highest interest rate loans.

✓ Don't co-sign for anyone else's credit card, to avoid putting your credit history at risk.

✓ Spend on your credit card today only what you can pay off tomorrow, to avoid getting caught in the "revolving credit card trap."

✓ Protect your credit card identity and use only secure sources when shopping, to avoid identity theft.

✓ Buy from need versus want or emotion, to avoid unnecessarily increasing your credit card debt.

✓ Only take credit cards with rewards or benefits that you need or will use, so that you are not paying extra for perceived rewards.

✓ Stay aware of your credit card balances, to avoid over limit fees.

Chapter 1: Smart Is a Relative Term

You are credit smart when you:

✓ Pay your balances in full each month.

✓ Don't take a store credit card just because they offer you a one-time percentage off of your first purchase.

✓ Use your debit card versus your credit card for most daily living purchases. Remember to keep track of purchases on your debit card so you don't get charged overdraft fees. Be aware of the differences in fraud liability for debit cards versus credit cards (discussed in Chapter 2), and monitor your statements for fraudulent purchases.

✓ Be aware of the APR on your credit cards, how and when your credit card statement cycles, and when your payment is due.

✓ Compare credit card rewards and benefits. Know what each card is really costing you.

Chapter 2: Not All Payments Are Created Equal

You are credit smart when you:

- ✓ Don't forget to look in your wallet to see what cards you carry and use most frequently.
- ✓ Evaluate your own credit smarts and reflect on your purchasing behaviors.
- ✓ Understand what cards you use every day.
- ✓ Decide which cards best fit in your life.
- ✓ Understand that there are different types of cards and know what benefits come from each type.
- ✓ Don't accept every card you are offered in the mail.
- ✓ Budget how you are going to use each type of card you have in your wallet.
- ✓ Know what your bank ATM limits are and communicate to your bank if your needs change.
- ✓ Leave balances available on your cards for rainy days or emergencies.

Chapter 3: Emotional Buying: How Your Emotions Are Being Manipulated to Make You Spend More

You are credit smart when you:

- ✓ Identify how you are feeling emotionally when you buy on your credit card.
- ✓ Stop and ask yourself when buying an item, "What is driving me emotionally to buy this?"
- ✓ Realize you are making an emotional purchase, and instead, take the same money and save it towards your dreams or goals.
- ✓ Don't spend any more on your card than you would pay with cash.

Chapter 4: Rewards Are Not Always Rewards: How to Make Your Credit Cards Work for You

You are credit smart when you:

- ✓ Don't overspend today to earn rewards tomorrow.
- ✓ Don't accept rewards offers and credit cards that you do not need or will not use.
- ✓ Track your earned rewards and use them before they expire.
- ✓ Ask yourself, "What is this reward really costing me?"
- ✓ Read the fine print on reward offers before you accept the credit card.

Chapter 5: Guess Who's Watching You Buy: Why?

You are credit smart when you:

- ✓ Are aware of all of the solicitations you receive in the mail, by email, and by phone.
- ✓ Are aware of recent purchases or purchase patterns that you believe triggered the solicitations you receive.
- ✓ Notice how you feel when you're bombarded with solicitations, whether they are for donations or are solicitations to buy cars or perfume.
- ✓ Understand that what you are buying and how you are buying is being tracked.
- ✓ Can link solicitations you receive with your purchasing methods and what you bought.
- ✓ Don't accept every store's frequent purchase cards.
- ✓ Don't fill out any online surveys.
- ✓ Don't give your email address to stores or restaurants.
- ✓ Check the box at the bottom of applications and warranty cards saying you do *not* want any future promotional materials.
- ✓ Think twice before you click on a pop-up offer when online and/or use a pop-up blocker on your internet browser to prevent these offers from appearing.

✓ Delete cookies (which are small files that are stored on your computer when you visit a website) from your computer on a regular basis to decrease the amount of information that can be tracked by websites while you are on the internet. This is a simple thing to do. If you don't know how, you can do a search on how to delete cookies from the internet browser that you use.

Chapter 6: To Be Credit Intelligent, It Is Critical to Know the Basics of Credit Scores

You are credit smart when you:

✓ Create and stay on a monthly budget.
✓ Avoid frequently applying for new credit cards and loans.
✓ Keep your oldest credit cards active. If you can, avoid closing credit card accounts you've had for a long time.
✓ Monitor your credit score and credit reports regularly.
✓ Pay your bills on time. This includes medical bills and utility contracts such as cell phones, cable bills, or satellite network contracts.
✓ Have at least 3 to 6 active accounts in different categories, i.e. major credit cards, gasoline cards, store cards, etc.
✓ Minimize the number of store credit cards you have in your name.
✓ Keep your credit card balances low. Paying down your credit card balances is a great way to help your credit score.
✓ Pay off your credit card balance with the highest interest rate before paying off lower interest rate balances. Continue to make payments on all of your balances to avoid damage to your credit score. After you have paid off the balance with the highest interest rate, take that amount and apply it to the balance with the next highest rate. By doing this, you will be amazed how quickly your balances will be paid in full.

✓ Make more than the minimum monthly payment required on your credit cards. Paying only the minimum amount each month will actually lower your credit score.

Chapter 7: There's No Free Lunch and There's No Quick Fix: Beware of Credit Repair Agencies

You are credit smart when you:

✓ Seek assistance from proven professionals such as a consumer credit counselor to assist you in improving your credit score.
✓ Take responsibility for improving your credit score and don't look to credit repair agencies or any other companies that promise a quick change in your score.

Chapter 8: Here's to Your Health: Take Action to Avoid Debt Stress

You are credit smart when you:

✓ Are aware of which physical symptoms relate to your credit card debt.
✓ Use positive coping mechanisms for dealing with stress.
✓ Take control of your money, instead of letting your money control you.
✓ Reach out for assistance to help alleviate stress and anxiety you may be feeling related to your credit card debt.

Chapter 9: Debt Can Kill Romance: Credit Problems Can Create Havoc in All of Your Relationships

You are credit smart when you:

- ✓ Learn about money management skills as a couple. This could include buying a book, ordering an audio course, or attending a seminar.
- ✓ Make a financial plan together.
- ✓ Create a bookkeeping system to track your expenses that works for both of you.
- ✓ Discuss your finances and expenses openly with your partner. Silence is not golden.
- ✓ Make new vows together to change your relationship with money.
- ✓ Determine spending limits together. This means that neither of you spends more than the maximum agreed amount without prior discussion and agreement between the two of you.

Chapter 10: The New Status Quo: Protecting Your Identity and Avoiding Online Shopping Perils

You are credit smart when you:

- ✓ Are mindful of identity fraud and how to protect yourself.
- ✓ Communicate to your card company if you plan to travel or if you are going to make a large or out-of-pattern credit card purchase.
- ✓ Shred all pre-approved credit card applications.
- ✓ Protect your Social Security number.
- ✓ Understand what recurring payments and auto-ship purchases are.
- ✓ Set limits around your online shopping.

Chapter 11: New Cards: Chip & PIN Cards Are Here to Stay

You are credit smart when you:

- ✓ Take the time to educate yourself on the advantages of the new Chip & PIN cards being issued.
- ✓ Make purchases using the Chip & PIN card, which gives you additional levels of security.
- ✓ Verify with your issuing bank that your Chip & PIN card can be easily utilized in the locations where you are traveling.
- ✓ Realize that all new payment programs have a learning curve.
- ✓ Check with your issuing bank for directions on when to shred your non-EMV cards.
- ✓ Activate the new cards and sign the signature panel as soon as they are received.
- ✓ Understand that PIN numbers will increase to 6 digits and that you should not use dates such as anniversaries and birthdays as your PIN.
- ✓ Understand that physical security remains your responsibility. Be sure to remove your card from the point-of-sale terminal at the end of transaction. Do *not* write your PIN number on your card.
- ✓ Pay attention to the instructions if you are using an ATM located outside of the United States. These instructions remind you to remove your card from the machine, because international ATMs do not automatically return to the card to you at the end of the transaction.
- ✓ Upon receiving your new Chip & PIN card in the mail, check for a new expiration date and/or possibly a new card number and communicate the new card data to any companies with whom you have set up automatic payments.
- ✓ Expect to see changes in the physical appearance of the plastic. Some issuers are no longer using raised, embossed numbers and letters.

Credit Intelligence Disclaimer

The information in this book, *Credit Intelligence*, is intended only to deepen your knowledge of the use and misuse of your credit cards and to help empower you to make good financial decisions. Any reliance you place on such information is therefore strictly at your own risk.

If you feel that you are in need of resolving any deep-seated issues associated with the use or misuse of your credit cards that may have been raised by any of the topics covered in this book, it may be appropriate for you to seek the counsel of a physician, licensed therapist, licensed counselor, social worker, attorney, or mental health professional.

None of the information provided in this book is intended to provide any medical, psychiatric, psychological, social work, legal, or any type of professional advice. None of the information is intended to replace or substitute for any information, opinions, recommendations, advice, or counseling provided by any legal, medical, psychiatric, psychological, counseling, or social work provider.

None of the information is intended to replace or be a substitute for any relationship that exists between a physician or health care professional and a patient, mental health professional and a patient, a mental health professional and a client, an attorney and a client, or a professional counselor and a client.

Any reliance you place on such information from any information contained in this book is therefore strictly at your own risk.

Credit Score Disclaimer

The credit reporting bureaus, most major credit card issuers, financial institutions, mortgage companies, etc. have all developed their own proprietary credit scoring models. Such proprietary credit scoring models are never fully published or disclosed.

As a result, any discussion of credit scores in this book is always a best guess estimate. It can be used to predict a reasonable range to approximate your credit score, but your own credit score may vary.

However, remember, your credit score is always directly related to your individual credit and debt activities. The same action taken by two credit card holders is likely to yield similar, but different, end results.

We make no representations or warranties of any kind, express or implied, about the completeness, accuracy, reliability, suitability, or availability, with respect to the information about any credit scores or how their values may change.

Any reliance you place on such information from any credit score information is therefore strictly at your own risk.

Reference Information Disclaimer

The reference indicators included in this book are for general information purposes only. The information on these external sources can be used to deepen your knowledge of the use and misuse of your credit cards and help empower you and the financial decisions you make.

However, we have no control over the accuracy, nature, content, or availability of information on any of these external sources. The inclusion of a reference indicator to any external source does not imply any recommendation or endorsement of the goods or services provided by the external source, the accuracy of the information, or the views expressed on the external source.

We make no representations or warranties of any kind, express or implied, about the completeness, accuracy, reliability, suitability, or availability with respect to the information obtained from any external source or the information, products, or services included therewith for any purpose.

Any reliance you place on such information from any external source is therefore strictly at your own risk.

Trademark Disclaimer

This book includes the trademarks of others. These trademarks are used under the legal doctrine of *Nominative Fair Use*, by which a person may use the trademark of another as a reference to describe a product or service. The trademarks used herein were used under the legal doctrine of Nominative Fair Use because: (1) the product or service could not be readily identified by the author without using the trademark; (2) the author only uses as much of the mark as is necessary for the identification; (3) the author has done nothing to suggest sponsorship or endorsement by the trademark holder or any actual connection to the trademark holder; (4) the author has not used the mark in a disparaging manner; and (5) since the trademark use is only nominative fair use, it cannot and does not dilute the corresponding trademark in any way. However, if any trademark owner desires that their trademark be removed from this publication, please contact the publisher. The publisher will make a reasonable effort to remove the corresponding trademark from future copies of the book.

About Polly Bauer

Credit and Payments Expert + CEO

Polly Bauer is the award-winning author of *The Plastic Effect*. She is founder of the Credit Card Loss Prevention School and CEO of Polly Bauer & Associates, a credit card consultancy she established in 1995.

Cyber Security professionals call her "a springboard for a new level of understanding of how credit cards are used and misused," and Knowledge Capital and Industry consultants praise her and her work because it's "filled with the wisdom that can only come from a true insider. No one knows the credit card industry better than Polly." She has identified sweeping industry trends in the fields of credit card fraud prevention and detection and, as a merchant advocate, specializes in loss prevention and customer payment data security.

As a key visionary and preeminent expert on credit cards operations and all forms of payment, Polly has directed the global expansion of e-commerce companies into 170 countries and currencies. She managed a $950 million credit card portfolio for a billion-dollar corporation.

Polly Bauer's genius is helping people to think before they swipe and teaching consumers to recognize the misconceptions they have about the use of credit. Her ability to strategically guide corporations *and* individuals through the maze of misinformation with true common sense, compassion, and humor is what sets her apart as an international corporate speaker, consumer advocate, and media expert. Her focus on credit cards and how it affects consumer purchasing behavior has been presented to audiences of thousands around the globe.

When she's not traveling and teaching, Polly loves to dance, go to movies, hit the beach with a good summer read, or get together with her husband, daughter, family, and friends.

Stay in touch with her and her growing tribe worldwide:

www.pollyabauer.com

Twitter: @PollyABauer

About Mava Heffler

Marketing and Communications Expert + CMO

Mava Heffler has a blue-chip background that includes marketing, advertising, communications, branding, market research, direct marketing, sponsorship, promotion, and public relations working at Fortune 500 leaders such as MasterCard International, Procter & Gamble, Johnson & Johnson, CNBC, and EMCOR Group, Inc.

Encompassing both domestic and international markets, Mava has expertise marketing to both consumers and businesses.

Having developed global branding and image campaigns, Mava has a depth of experience creating enterprise-wide, integrated marketing strategies, core competencies, and restaging business units. With an intrinsic ability to weave together corporate vision, strategic planning, creativity, and marketing execution, Mava produces breakthrough results.

Named a "Brand Builder," one of the "Top Women in Business to Watch," and listed amongst "Top Marketers" by the press and media, Mava's programs have received a variety of industry awards. She has been broadly quoted in the press and the media, and has been a frequent presenter at events and conferences.

On the personal side, Mava enjoys spending quality time with her daughter, friends, and family, as well as snow skiing, scuba diving, and travel.

End Notes

Introduction

[1] Mottola, Gary, "In Our Best Interest: Women, Financial Literacy and Credit Card Behavior," FINRA Investor Educational Foundation, (April 2012), http://www.finrafoundation.org/web/groups/foundation/@foundation/documents/foundation/p125971.pdf.

[2] Reh, F. John, "Pareto's Principle: The 80-20 Rule," About.com Money, (2015), http://management.about.com/cs/generalmanagement/a/Pareto081202.htm.

Chapter 2

[3] Polly A. Bauer and Stephen Lesavich. *The Plastic Effect: How Urban Legends Influence the Use and Misuse of Credit Cards.* (Coconut Avenue, Inc., 2012): 164-166. Reprinted with permission Coconut Avenue, Inc.

[4] Curry, Pat, "10 questions before getting secured credit cards," (2012), http://www.bankrate.com/finance/credit-cards/10-questions-before-getting-a-secured-credit-card-1.aspx

[5] Bauer and Lesavich, *The Plastic Effect,* (Coconut Avenue, Inc., 2012): 175-76.

[6] Regulation E, pursuant to the Electronic Fund Transfer Act (EFTA), 12 C.F.R. §205.6 sets liability of consumer for unauthorized transfers, Federal Deposit Insurance Corporation, accessed June 15, 2015, www.fdic.gov/regulations/laws/rules/6500-3100.html#fdic6500205.6.

[7] Reagan, Rebecca S. and Aaron M. Thompson, "Credit CARD Act Requirements for Gift Certificates, Store Gift Cards, and General-Use Prepaid Cards," *Consumer Compliance Outlook,* (First Quarter 2013), https://www.consumercomplianceoutlook.org/2013/first-quarter/credit-card-act-requirements-gift-certicicates-gift-cards-prepaid-cards/.

[8] Federal Trade Commission, "Consumer Information: Gift Cards," (2012), https://www.consumer.ftc.gov/articles/0182-gift-cards.

Chapter 3

[9] Thau, Barbara, "'Buy Me!' 7 Ways Stores Get You to Make an Impulse Purchase," *DailyFinance*, (April 26, 2012), http://www.dailyfinance.com/2012/04/26/buy-me-7-ways-stores-get-you-to-make-an-impulse-purchase/.

[10] Mannino, Naomi, "7 shopping secrets retailers won't tell you," *Bankrate*, accessed May 11, 2015, http://www.bankrate.com/finance/personal-finance/7-shopping-secrets-retailers-won-t-tell-you-5.aspx.

[11] Leamy, Elizabeth, "How to Watch Out for Fake Sales," *ABC News*, (January 31, 2012), http://abcnews.go.com/Business/buyer-beware-shoppers-wise-fake-sales/story?id=15475097.

[12] SAGE Publications, "When self-esteem is threatened, people pay with credit cards," accessed May 11, 2015, *ScienceDaily*, www.sciencedaily.com/releases/2011/05/110505181541.htm.

Chapter 5

[13] Duhigg, Charles, "How Companies Learn Your Secrets," *New York Times Magazine*, (February 16, 2012), http://www.nytimes.com/2012/02/19/magazine/shopping-habits.html?pagewanted=all&_r=0.

[14] Lutz, Ashley and Matt Townsend, "Big Brother Is Watching You Shop," *Bloomberg Business*, (December 15, 2011), http://www.bloomberg.com/bw/magazine/big-brother-is-watching-you-shop-12152011.html.

Chapter 6

[15] Bauer and Lesavich, *The Plastic Effect*, (Coconut Avenue, Inc., 2012): 38.

[16] Obringer, Lee Ann, "How Credit Scores Work," *Learning Source*, February 16, 2006, http://learningsource.org/Math/creditscoredetail.aspx.

[17] Bauer and Lesavich, *The Plastic Effect*, (Coconut Avenue, Inc., 2012): 39.

[18] Bauer and Lesavich, *The Plastic Effect*, (Coconut Avenue, Inc., 2012): 38.

[19] Steiner, Stenya, "How Your Credit Score Affects Your Mortgage Rate," *Bankrate*, (Updated June 2, 2015), http://www.bankrate.

com/finance/mortgages/how-credit-scores-impact-your-mortgage-rate-1.aspx.

20 Detweiler, Gerri, "What Credit Score Do I Need to Buy a Car?" *credit.com News*, (September 12, 2014), http://www.bankrate. com/finance/mortgages/how-credit-scores-impact-your-mortgage-rate-1.aspx.

Chapter 8

21 Wolff, Sarah, "The State of Lending in America & its Impact on U.S. Households," Center for Responsible Lending, (December 2012), http://www.responsiblelending.org/state-of-lending/reports/5-Credit-Cards.pdf.

22 Traub, Amy and Catherine Reutschlein, "The Plastic Safety Net: 2012," *Demos*, (May 22, 2012), http://www.demos.org/publication/plastic-safety-net.

23 Harris Poll for National Foundation for Credit Counseling, "The 2014 Financial Literacy Survey," (2014), https://www.nfcc.org/NewsRoom/FinancialLiteracy/files2013/NFCC_2014Financial LiteracySurvey datasheet and key findings 031314%20FINAL.pdf.

24 American Psychological Association, "Stress in America: Are Teens Adopting Adults' Stress Habits?" (February 11, 2014): 7, http://www.apa.org/news/press/releases/stress/2013/stress-report.pdf.

25 Ibid, Page 7.

26 American Psychological Association, "Stress in America: Paying With Our Health," (February 4, 2015): 7, http://www.apa.org/news/press/releases/stress/2014/stress-report.pdf.

27 Dugan, Andrew and Stephanie Kafka, "Student Debt Linked to Worse Health and Less Wealth," *Gallup*, (August 7, 2014), http://www.gallup.com/poll/174317/student-debt-linked-worse-health-less-wealth.aspx.

28 American Psychological Association, "Stress in America: Are Teens Adopting Adults' Stress Habits?" (February 11, 2014): 10, http://www.apa.org/news/press/releases/stress/2013/stress-report.pdf.

29 Mayo Clinic, "Chronic stress puts your health at risk," accessed June 8, 2015, http://www.mayoclinic.org/healthy-living/stress-management/in-depth/stress/art-20046037.

30 Mientka, Matthew, "The Effects of Debt Reach Further Than Just Stress; Include Heart Disease, Stroke, and Mental Illness," *Medical Daily*, (July 13, 2014), http://www.medicaldaily.com/effects-debt-reach-further-just-stress-include-heart-disease-stroke-and-mental-illness-292720.

[31] American Psychological Association, "Stress in America: Paying With Our Health," (February 4, 2015): 31, http://www.apa.org/news/press/releases/stress/2014/stress-report.pdf.

[32] Bouchez, Collette, "Can Stress Cause Weight Gain?" *WebMD*, (May 13, 2005), http://www.webmd.com/diet/can-stress-cause-weight-gain?page=2.

[33] Iliades, Chris, "Living with IBS and GERD," *Everyday Health*, (August 23, 2013), http://www.everydayhealth.com/ibs/living-with-ibs-and-gerd.aspx.

[34] Mientka, Matthew, "The Effects of Debt Reach Further Than Just Stress; Include Heart Disease, Stroke, and Mental Illness," *Medical Daily*, (July 13, 2014), http://www.medicaldaily.com/effects-debt-reach-further-just-stress-include-heart-disease-stroke-and-mental-illness-292720.

[35] American Psychological Association, "Stress in America: Are Teens Adopting Adults' Stress Habits?" (February 11, 2014): 19, http://www.apa.org/news/press/releases/stress/2013/stress-report.pdf.

[36] Richardson, Thomas, Peter Elliott, and Ronald Roberts, "The relationship between personal unsecured debt and mental and physical health: A systematic review and meta-analysis," *Clinical Psychology Review* 33:8 (December 2013): 1148, http://www.sciencedirect.com/science/article/pii/S0272735813001256.

[37] Sherman, Chuck, "Debt and Depression," Human Service Agency, accessed June 15, 2015, http://www.humanserviceagency.org/library/MH-Sherman-Debt%20and%20Depression.pdf.

[38] Robinson, Lawrence, Jeanne Segal, and Melinda Smith, "How Exercise Benefits Depression, Anxiety, and Stress: Using Physical Activity to Improve Your Mental Health," *HelpGuide.org*, (April 2015), http://www.helpguide.org/articles/exercise-fitness/emotional-benefits-of-exercise.htm.

[39] American Psychological Association, "Stress in America: Paying With Our Health," (February 4, 2015): 7, http://www.apa.org/news/press/releases/stress/2014/stress-report.pdf.

[40] Renter, Elizabeth, "The Dark Link Between Financial Stress and Depression," *US News & World Report Health*, (February 25, 2015), http://health.usnews.com/health-news/health-wellness/articles/2015/02/25/the-dark-link-between-financial-stress-and-depression.

[41] Bortz, Daniel, "Surviving the Emotional Toll of Bankruptcy," *US News & World Report Money*, (January 18, 2013), http://money.usnews.com/money/personal-finance/articles/2013/01/18/surviving-the-emotional-toll-of-bankruptcy.

⁴² Donatelle, Rebecca, *My Health: An Outcomes Approach*, (Pearson Education, Inc., 2015), http://www.pearsonhighered.com/donatelle1einfo/myhealth/assets/images/other/Donatelle_Ch03.pdf.

⁴³ Collingwood, Jane, "The Power of Music To Reduce Stress," *PsychCentral*, (January 30, 2013), http://psychcentral.com/lib/the-power-of-music-to-reduce-stress/000930.

⁴⁴ Jacobe, Dennis, "One in Three Americans Prepare a Detailed Household Budget," *Gallup*, (June 3, 2013), http://www.gallup.com/poll/162872/one-three-americans-prepare-detailed-household-budget.aspx.

⁴⁵ Consumer Financial Protection Bureau, "Key Dimensions and Processes in the U.S. Credit Reporting System: A review of how the nation's largest credit bureaus manage consumer data," (December 2012): 16, http://files.consumerfinance.gov/f/201212_cfpb_credit-reporting-white-paper.pdf.

⁴⁶ Bauer and Lesavich, *The Plastic Effect*, (Coconut Avenue, Inc., 2012): 25-35.

⁴⁷ ADI News Services, "Beware of plastic zombies," *Arizona Daily Independent*, (August 6, 2013), https://arizonadailyindependent.com/2013/08/06/beware-of-plastic-zombies/.

⁴⁸ Bauer and Lesavich, *The Plastic Effect*, (Coconut Avenue, Inc., 2012): 119-120.

Chapter 10

⁴⁹ National Crime Prevention Council, "Tips to Prevent Identity Theft," (2015), http://www.ncpc.org/topics/fraud-and-identity-theft/tips-to-prevent-identity-theft.

⁵⁰ TransUnion, "How to Prevent Identity Theft," (2015), http://www.transunion.com/personal-credit/identity-theft-and-fraud/how-to-prevent-identity-theft.page.

⁵¹ Bauer and Lesavich, *The Plastic Effect*, (Coconut Avenue, Inc., 2012): 177.

Chapter 11

⁵² Cardwerk, "History of smart cards," accessed June 15, 2015, http://www.cardwerk.com/smartcards/smartcard_history.aspx.

⁵³ Gemalto, "Milestone: Four Million Students Now Use University Smart Cards Developed by Gemalto and Santander Universities Global Division," accessed June 15, 2015, http://www.gemalto.com/press/Pages/news_658.aspx.